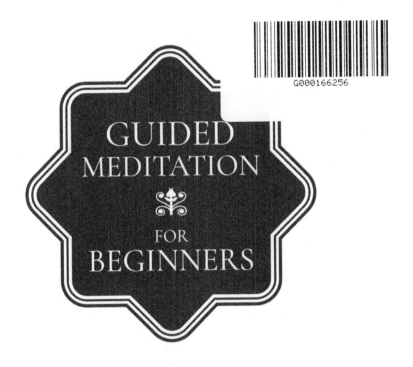

GUIDED MEDITATION FOR BEGINNERS

A Guide To Becoming Happier In 10 Days Thanks To Practical Meditation: Highly Effective Techniques For Anxiety, Unlock Chakra Awakening And Get More Deep Sleep.

ASANA SWAMI & RICHARD REIKIVIC

Edited in Europe, printed in the United States of America unless otherwise specified.

ASIN/ISBN CODE: 9798617296503
Library of Congress Control Number: 2020902703 (LCCN)

www.youbookseditions.com

# Download the Audio Book Version of This Book for FREE

If you love listening to audiobooks on-the-go, I have great news for you. You can download the audiobook version of this book for **FREE** just by signing up for a **FREE** 30-day Audible trial! See below for more details!

## Audible Trial Benefits

As an audible customer, you will receive the below benefits with your 30-day free trial:

- FREE audible book copy of this book
- After the trial, you will get 1 credit each month to use on any audiobook
- Your credits automatically roll over to the next month if you don't use them
- Choose from Audible's 200,000 + titles
- Listen anywhere with the Audible app across multiple devices
- Make easy, no-hassle exchanges of any audiobook you don't love
- Keep your audiobooks forever, even if you cancel your membership
- And much more

# SCAN THE QR CODE AND GET YOUR FREE AUDIBLE BOOK

## US LISTENER

## UK LISTENER

## FR LISTENER

## DE LISTENER

# Table of Contents

# Introduction

At the point when you are up to speed in the passionate change of insatiability, outrage, and daydream, you may end up capitulating to some genuine physical infirmities; and when you are sick, the world may appear to be an extremely grim spot. Saying this doesn't imply that, in any case, that the entirety of our ailments is because of outrageous feelings. Introduction to substances to which you might be hypersensitive can modify every little thing about you.

It can cause vicious emotional episodes, misery, fantasies, and a wide range of physical impacts, including real tissue harm. Whatever the reason, the ailment is regularly joined by a variety of problematic feelings. Projects that have been intended to utilize unwinding strategies and reflection have been demonstrated to be viable in controlling both the physical impacts and the feelings which go with them. However, as gainful as they might be, such techniques can take one just a step forward up until now.

## The Prevalence Psychophysiological Effects of Meditation

The famous Russian physiologist Pavlov (1849–1936) accentuated the job that the brain and cerebrum play in physiology. From the start, one may accept this to be just an announcement of certainty, since that piece of the mind is typically thought to include little else other than intuition. It partakes in the creation of numerous hormones, both straightforwardly and in a roundabout way.

Each part of an individual is interrelated, and that is how and why contemplations and feelings can have such a broad impact. That is, nonetheless, additionally why contemplation and quiet actuating musings can be so balancing out thus solid. One can securely accept, at that point, that a large portion of what adds to legitimate working likewise adds to great wellbeing.

## Helpful Hints for Better Practice and Better Health

As you progress in your training, you are required to sit unmoving for more and longer timeframes at a stretch. It is then that some significant physical restrictions may oblige you to make a few changes in the manner that you set. Should you decide to disregard them, imagining that there is only one right approach to rehearse, you may cause yourself unnecessary agony and interruption (which implies that you won't have the option to focus); and you may conceivably open yourself to hopeless physical harm too.

It isn't abnormal for individuals who have gone on retreats to come back with agonizingly harmed knees, having held a situation regardless of agony, and having respected the following deadness, mainly because they have more issues than they can cure. To reword the Kalama Sutra, "Don't accomplish something since you have been told to do as such, however, give it and locate a shot how it functions for you." Be consistently on watch for what doesn't appear to be right, and see what may be done about it. Many numerous techniques can be attempted. There is no motivation to need to submit to torment or altogether debility, particularly when no good thing can happen to it.

# Chapter 1: Demystifying Anxiety

## What Is Anxiety?

At its core, anxiety can be defined as a feeling that presents itself as overwhelmingly worrisome. Other words that can be used to describe anxiety include fear, an undefinable tension in the gut, and even excessive nervousness. It's important to understand that in small doses, anxiety is normal. Everyone experiences anxiety due to the pressures of everyday life. This is not uncommon. What is uncommon is when an individual feel anxious on almost a constant basis. Today, it's estimated that over 40 millions Americans suffer from some sort of anxiety disorder.

## Anxiety Is Not Always Equal

Another important distinction that needs to be made about anxiety from the onset is that the World Health Organization has determined that not all countries experience anxiety equally. For example, it's estimated that the countries with the highest levels of anxiety include the following:

1. India
2. China
3. The United States
4. Brazil
5. Indonesia

Contrasting, the countries with the lowest levels of anxiety include the following:

1. Denmark
2. Finland
3. The Netherlands
4. Sweden
5. Ireland

While the highest and lowest levels of anxiety may exist in a particular country for a variety of reasons, it's incredibly interesting to note that higher levels of anxiety can be seen in different parts of the world. This makes anxiety a phenomenon that can change depending on where you live. It also makes anxiety something that can be cured. Understanding this is the first step in curing your anxiety, as long as you are willing to lessen certain things in your life that cause stress in the first place.

## The Discovery of Stress

The ancient Greeks were the first people to discover anxiety, which shouldn't be too much of a surprise considering they are responsible for discovering much of life's most basic principles to this day. When the Greeks first recognized anxiety, however, they did not immediately give it this name. Instead, they described it using the word hysteric. Specifically, the ancient

Greek term for hysteria was *hysterika*, which can be directly translated to mean uterus. This makes sense, as in those days it was determined that only women were affected by the hysteria that anxiety brought with it. Specifically, the ancient Greeks determined that a uterus produced an excess of female semen when a female was not having enough sex in her life. For this reason, it was thought that the only remedy to this ailment was for a woman to engage in more sexual relations as a way to release the hysteria that her semen was producing.

## Hysteria Through the Years

After the Greeks officially coined a term for stress, other cultures throughout history also came into contact as well. One way that this is apparent is by taking a look at the events of the Salem Witch Trials. These trials took place from the 1500s until the late 1720s. Women, in particular, were seen to be witches when they possessed irrationally high levels of hysteria. A similar phenomenon occurred in the Victorian era in Britain, where women were often taken to insane asylums if they had panic attacks or had other anxiety-related issues. It's not clear whether men can suffer from anxiety until the Civil War when post-traumatic stress disorder was diagnosed amongst soldiers. By the early 1900s, the Russians were the first country to treat their soldiers on the battlefield with psychiatrists who went to war with the rest of the military. Finally, we come to the present day, where anxiety is frequently combatted using anxiety medication and antidepressants.

## Where Does Anxiety Come From?

If you think about it, anxiety today is far different from anxiety that existed for people living in historical times. For example, not many of us have to worry about hunting our food. If someone goes hunting, they are typically doing it as a sport, not because it's how they survive. Anxiety exists because our ancestors had to deal with stressors related to their livelihood. They could be easily attacked if they weren't on high alert, or if they weren't protecting themselves properly. In this way, it's easy to see how the body used anxiety to bring greater awareness to a person's surroundings. Today, our anxiety is different than what it was when it was first being used by humans. We may have anxiety because we're worried we're going to lose our job, or we have emotional family problems that we have to deal with.

## How Does Anxiety Feel?

Even though you might know that you have a lot of anxiety regularly, it still might be difficult to define it on your terms. On average, people who have some sort of anxiety problem experience these feelings regularly:

1.  **Excessive worrying:** This worrying might come from watching the news, or it might turn on whenever your child leaves the house. The worrisome thoughts will not go away, no matter how hard you try to make them disappear.
2.  **Muscle cramps:** Another sign that you might have too much anxiety is if your muscles often feel cramped or tight. This tension can form in the jaw, through clenching your fists or even biting the inside of your cheek. You might think that these are simply bad habits you need to break, but the fact of the matter is that it could be a sign that you suffer from anxiety.
3.  **An unbalanced gut:** Irritable Bowel Syndrome, also known as IBS, often goes hand-in-hand with anxiety. Even though you may have never thought about it, your gut is quite sensitive when you feel anxiety coming on. Other digestive issues other than IBS can also be the result of anxiety. Even a simple upset stomach can be a sign that you are experiencing more anxiety than usual.

## The First Signs That Anxiety Is Coming

These 3 can be seen as the most common signs of anxiety, but other, less noticeable, signs can also tell you that you are experiencing it. These first signs include:

1. Shortness of breath
2. A feeling of lightheadedness
3. A headache or migraine
4. Sweating, especially if it's not hot out
5. A pounding in your heart

Again, anxiety is quite common. Everyone experiences the first signs of anxiety from time to time, but you may still want to lessen anxiety in your life whenever you can. We all want to lead a stress-free and happy life, and sometimes our anxiety can make this seem impossible. Understanding the history of anxiety can help to show that anxiety has been around since the beginning of time. Our body naturally produces anxiety as a way to tell our brain that our body may be in danger. There are plenty of ways to reduce anxiety, and it's important to realize that anxiety is something that you can control to some degree. With the right guidance and knowledge, you will soon be able to lessen anxiety in your life positively and permanently.

## Stress and the Physical Body

This chapter is going to discuss how stress can influence the body, and what the brain is doing during the times when you feel the most stress in your life. After reading this chapter, you will have a basic understanding of the body's processes when you are undergoing high levels of stress. By being able to identify how your body reacts to stress, you should be able to recognize when you are feeling more anxious than usual. If you can understand this, you can then take a step back when you are in a stressful situation and possibly calm yourself down before a panic attack or another sign of anxiety strikes.

# The Hypothalamus and the Body's Nervous Systems

Within the body, there exist 2 types of nervous systems that have to do with stress. Collectively, they are known as the autonomic nervous system. Separately, they are known as the parasympathetic nervous system, and the sympathetic nervous system. While both are certainly important aspects of the human body, the sympathetic nervous system is going to be more important for our discussion; however, understanding what the parasympathetic nervous system does is still important. The parasympathetic nervous system is primarily responsible for the regulation of various parts of our bodily functions. Some of these functions include:

1. Regulating digestion
2. Keeping the heart rate down
3. Regulating the intestinal system

In contrast to the functions of the parasympathetic nervous system, the sympathetic nervous system does the opposite. You have probably heard of the sympathetic nervous system before but may not know it. The sympathetic nervous system is also known as your body's "fight or flight response." In other words, it produces your body's responses when you feel like you are in a stressful or potentially threatening circumstance. These responses directly contrast the functions of the parasympathetic nervous system. When in harmony, these 2 nervous systems balance the body, but when you are feeling tense, this balance becomes completely out of sync. Your fight or flight response is what kicks your anxiety into high alert. Often, a person like you or me may not even be able to tell that the body is automatically going into fight or flight. For this reason, you must be aware of the signs that will tell you when this occurs.

### Signs of Fight or Flight Response

Signs that your fight or flight response has started include the following:

### Sign #1: Developing Tunnel Vision

When this happens, it's almost as if you cannot see out of your peripheral vision. Dizziness or being able to only focus on one thing at a time can accompany a tunnel-vision reaction to something.

### Sign #2: Greater Sensitivity to Noise

Another, subtle, sign that your body has gone into fight or flight is if you notice that you can hear noises that are low in volume or intensity.

### Sign #3: Enlarged Pupils

If you see someone with pupils that are larger than normal, especially when it's perfectly bright outside, this can be one indicator that their body feels particularly stressed at that moment. You can think about the sympathetic nervous system as being connected to our most primal feelings of safety. Before the days when electricity and lighting were easily accessible, the human body needed to adapt to certain situations when there was an immediate threat within their vicinity. One of the ways to do this was to heighten vision through an enlargement of the pupils.

### Sign #4: Pale and Chilly Skin

When your sympathetic nervous system is pumping out cortisol in high doses, this means that it's using energy that would otherwise be used to do things such as heat the body and provide it with a vital glow. Instead of this energy being used to heat the body, it's going to be used to provide more energy to your extremities, eyes, and ears. This way, your body will be on high alert in case it needs to act and move quickly.

### Sign #5: A Dry Mouth

Another telltale sign that you are experiencing stress and that your sympathetic nervous system has begun to work overtime is that your mouth is going to feel excessively dry. This is especially true if your body is in the process of digesting something that you recently ate. Similar to when the body saves its energy and causes you to look paler and feel cooler, it's also going to stop digesting food if an immediate stressor becomes apparent. With the stoppage of digestion will come the stoppage of saliva to the mouth, which will result in a dry sensation.

### Physical Signs of Stress Over Long-Term

As you can see from the examples of what happens when your body's fight or flight response is triggered, your body is going to change when it's under a lot of anxiety. When these changes are brief, there's not a whole lot of problems that will occur over the long term. The body is hard-wired to experience and deal with anxiety now and then, so it will be able to handle high levels of stress in small doses. On the other hand, problems that can have longer effects on the body can occur if we allow ourselves to undergo large levels of stress over a long time. Some of the physical signs that your body is experiencing stress too frequently include the following:

*Sign #1: General Fatigue*

General fatigue can be best defined as feeling tired during the day even when you have got a good night's sleep the night before. You can also experience general fatigue if you feel tired during the evening when you are trying to go to sleep, but cannot seem to fall asleep, no matter how hard you try.

*Sign #2: Weight Gain or Loss*

Any type of weight gain or weight loss can indicate to you that your body is experiencing stress too often. This is especially true if there are no other reasons why you are gaining or losing weight. For example, sometimes people gain or lose weight because they recently experienced a death in the family or because they are going through a tough breakup. These are normal reasons for a weight change. If you do not have anything going on in your life that would lead to a change in your weight, then general anxiety may be the cause.

### Sign #3: You Are Getting Sick Often

When your fight or flight response has been turned on, it's going to require more energy than normal so that it can heighten your senses. When this happens, it means that it's going to take energy away from other systems in order body to get the energy that it needs. One area of the body that it takes energy away from is your immune system. When your immune system is down, it's much more likely that you will become sick, with a common cold, the flu, or another type of bacteria that can enter the body.

## The Effects of Anxiety on Our Reproductive Organs

Again, it's important to understand that everyone is going to experience anxiety in their life at one time or another, but excessive stress is what you should be looking to avoid. In addition to the potential problems that were just discussed above, some problems that can occur particularly in men include erectile dysfunction and sometimes even complete impotence. For women, the most common sign of excessive anxiety via the reproductive organs is a light or sometimes non-existent menstrual cycle. This can sometimes even lead to more worrying for a woman since a lighter period is also an early sign of pregnancy.

As should be obvious after reading this chapter, many different types of phenomena take place in the body in reaction to high levels of anxiety. It's not uncommon for people to simply not notice when these things are happening inside of them; however, if you have ever felt your body reacting to anxiety in one of the ways that were mentioned above, then you already have an awareness of how uncomfortable this can be. Having a grounded, fully functioning body is one of the key fundamental elements of leading a healthy life; yet as our environments become increasingly filled with stress, functioning within a stressful environment sometimes seems like it's becoming the norm instead of the exception. This is not normal, and you should constantly be working against feeling like it is.

# Signs That Indicate You Are Suffering From Anxiety

While the information previously presented is helpful when you are seeking to understand how anxiety influences the body from a biological perspective, the truth of the matter is that it can be hard to identify the changes that are taking place within the body, especially if you are stressed while they are occurring. For example, it can be a bit difficult to notice that your skin has become paler and chillier to the touch, especially if you haven't had the time to look at yourself in a mirror. Following will be presented an outline of some of the more obvious signs that can exist when your anxiety is taking a noticeable toll on you. These signs will include ones that have to do with your mental state, your relationships, and even your ability to complete tasks daily.

### The Mental Signs of Anxiety

Before we get into other aspects of your life that anxiety can negatively influence, we will begin by examining the mind. One of the first ways that you may personally notice heightened levels of anxiety that are affecting you is through your internal monologue with yourself. Some of the mental signs that can indicate that stress is taking a toll on you include the following:

### Sign #1: Restlessness

If you have ever laid in bed for what seems like hours on end, with your mind constantly racing, then you have experienced the side-effect of stress that is restlessness. This can often be one of the first indicators that stress is taking a toll on your mind in the form of overactive and constant thoughts. In contrast, if you are experiencing the desire to sleep too much, this too can be a sign of excessive anxiety. Remember, when you are stressed, your body is going to be using energy disproportionately. This can certainly cause you to feel more tired than normal. Lastly, restlessness does not necessarily mean that you are either not sleeping or sleeping too much. Restlessness can also manifest itself as causing you to sleep for just a few hours, before waking up or tossing and turning throughout the night.

### Sign #2: Irritability

Of course, if you are having trouble sleeping, this can certainly result in feeling increasingly irritable on a day-to-day basis. The biggest way that irritability can negatively affect someone who is experiencing stress is through their relationships. Often, irritable people do not even notice that they are irritable because they are only irritable when they are around others. When they are alone, everything appears to be fine. If you are worried that you might be projecting irritability onto others, you should try to look inward and diagnose your irritability. This way, you can at least attempt to be more pleasant around the people that you care about and interact with often.

### Sign #3: Compulsive Behaviors

Even though compulsive behaviors can be considered actions rather than thoughts, this type of behavior often comes from a place of mental instability. For example, if you are subconsciously stressing about leaving your house for one reason or another, this may result in you feeling like you must meticulously clean your house before doing so. The compulsion to clean your house is a behavioral response to the mental anxiety that you are experiencing, rather than a behavior in its own right.

### Sign #4: Forgetfulness

Forgetfulness can be similar to compulsive behavior because forgetting to do something can be just as compulsive as repetitive behavior. For example, let's say that you are someone who still has anxiety about leaving your house, but instead of cleaning, you forget to bring something along with you after you have already left the house instead. This can result in you feeling like you must go back to your house, and then ultimately makes you feel like you have wasted so much time that there's no point in leaving the house again. This means that if you typically categorize yourself as a forgetful person, it might be wise to look inward in an attempt to figure out whether you are truly forgetting, or if some other mental stress is lying just beneath the surface.

### Sign #5: Memory Problems

Forgetfulness is different from experiencing memory problems. When you are experiencing memory problems, you will likely have difficulty recalling events that have taken place over the short term. Often, a traumatic event is also going to trigger memory loss, because the brain is trying to protect itself from experiencing this pain repeatedly. Additionally, it's important to note that what can initially be restlessness can turn into memory issues, because being tired can often result in the brain lacking its memory capabilities.

## Relationship-Related Signs of Anxiety

In addition to personal symptoms of anxiety that can exist in the mind, when you are feeling anxious frequently, the health of your relationships will also likely be compromised. For some of us, the deterioration of our relationships can sometimes be even more devastating than the mental unclarity that is coming to light. When we see people whom we love pulling away from us, it can be understandably scary and cause even more anxiety to come to the forefront of our brains than already exists. For this reason, it's important to be able to notice when your actions may be indicating that your anxiety is causing your relationships to become potentially jeopardized. The signs that anxiety could be ruining your relationships include the following:

### Sign #1: You are "Vegging Out" More than You Are Going Out

One of the first indicators that stress is causing you to back away from your relationships can often be if you suddenly are less excited about spending time with others. For example, if you typically spend most of your weekends out and about with friends, but have noticed that you are spending a lot more time alone lately, then this can be a sign that anxiety is plaguing your normal relationship habits. Sure, if you are going through a breakup or have had some other stressful situation recently occur, then it's perhaps normal for you to feel yourself pulling away from others for at least a little while. On the other hand, if you can recognize that this shift in your behavior is something that is slowly becoming the norm rather than the exception, it might be time to either seek professional help or determine what the root cause of this stress is so that you can rectify the situation in which you find yourself.

### Sign #2: An Underactive Libido

We touched on this briefly previously, but another surefire sign that anxiety is making your relationships more difficult is if you are experiencing problems in the bedroom. For example, you might be trying to please your partner in the bedroom, but often come away from the sexual experience feeling like you were simply going through the motions the entire time it was occurring. This can be frightening for any relationship, especially because a decline in sexual satisfaction is one of the first signs that a relationship might be in trouble. It's important to understand that just because you do not necessarily feel physically attracted to your partner, this does not mean that your relationship is going to fall apart. Anxiety can often cloud our ability to love our partner adequately, but this does not mean that this feeling of unattraction will last forever.

### Sign #3: Moodiness

Another sign that anxiety might be taking more of a toll on you than you initially thought is if you are finding that more than one person has commented on your moodiness. Of course, when someone tells you that you are being moody, you may initially become defensive or want to become argumentative with that person; however, if more than one person is informing you that they believe you are being moodier than usual, you may want to start being receptive to what they are saying. This is especially true if you are typically not moody. No one wants to be around someone who is constantly changing their emotional demeanor. Additionally, people sometimes will jump to the irrational conclusion that they are developing a bipolar disorder, based on their moodiness. Before you start self-diagnosing yourself with a mental illness, the more appropriate action would be to try and figure out if your moodiness is associated with your anxiety.

### Miscellaneous Signs of Anxiety

In addition to the mental and relationship-related anxiety signs that we've already discussed, there are a few other warning signs that can suggest you have got too much anxiety on your plate. These symptoms can manifest themselves in the following ways:

1. **Obsessing over irrational fears:** If you have ever met someone with a phobia, then you know someone who lives with irrational fear. While irrational fears are often fears that began when an individual was young, excessive worrying is also often associated with older people who have too much time on their hands. This is similar to become stir crazy after being in your house for too long time. These days, irrational fears can seem even more apparent than ever before, for the simple reason that the news seems to love featuring sensationalistic stories.

2. **Experiencing panic attacks:** People can experience panic attacks for a variety of reasons, but at their core, they are typically caused by either a need that is not being met in a person's life or the realization of something during a stressful time. These types of attacks can often

last for minutes and are accompanied by difficulty breathing, stomach cramps, and even an excessive heart rate. It's important to note that just because you have 1 or 2 panic attacks, this does not mean that you have a serious issue that needs to be addressed; rather, you may simply be going through a particularly difficult period in your life and need to cope with these issues more directly.

3. **Experiencing flashbacks:** Lastly, anxiety can often come from experiences from the past that have left a lasting impression on the mind and body of a person. This is especially true if that experience negatively manipulated not just the mind of the person, but also touched the individual's physical body in some manner. We will discuss the various types of anxiety disorders later on, but flashbacks are often related to serious trauma that has occurred in a person's life.

When you are self-examining your mental tendencies, it can become strangely satisfying to determine that you are guilty of all of them and have an anxiety disorder. Before reaching that conclusion, you should try and examine your behavior over a longer time. For example, you can try documenting your behavioral tendencies for between 2 weeks to a month. This will allow you to determine whether the behavior you are experiencing is consistent, or it's just something that will pass soon.

## The Many Causes of Anxiety

It's simply misguided to say that people who suffer from high levels of anxiety are living their lives incorrectly. As you will see, there are a variety of factors at work that can lead a person to feel as if their anxiety is too difficult to endure.

### Environmental Factors

In many cases, your environment is going to determine the degree to which your anxiety affects you, regardless of the severity of your anxiety within your brain. In other words, if you grow up in an environment where experiencing anxiety is not a common occurrence, then it's unlikely that you will develop anxiety-motivated tendencies. Additionally, your environment alone can cause you to develop an anxiety-related disorder, even if you are not genetically pre-dispositioned to develop one. There are plenty of studies out there that suggest that it's entirely possible to cure anxiety disorders without the use of medicine at all. It's been proven that it's possible to rectify some of the effects of stress through environmental and behavioral changes alone.

It's obvious that a stressful home environment is going to likely cause a person environmental stress, but it's less obvious that environmental stress can also come from changes in your environment as well. A huge example of an environmental stressor that over 50% of the US population has experienced is the stress that comes with going through a divorce. When you divorce someone, you are forced to completely change and alter the way of life that you are used to living. With divorce also comes concerns about money, children, and even where both parties will live. This is a great example of how changes in your environment can lead to great levels of stress. At the core of this type of stress often lies the desire to feel safe, secure, and loved by the people around you and the ones whom you call your family. Feeling safe is a biological need that all humans have, and this is where much environmental anxiety begins to take form.

# The Emotional Causes of Anxiety

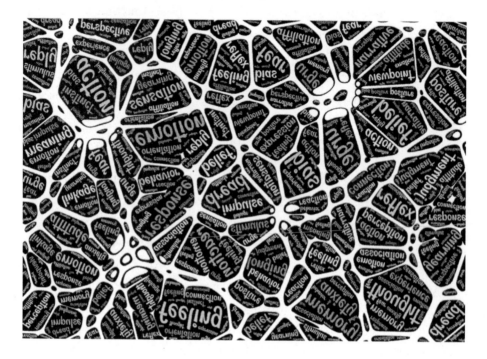

In addition to our physical surroundings causing stress, another way that anxiety can manifest is through our emotions. Emotions have to do with our interactions with other people, how we were raised, and how we feel we should be loved. A major way that our emotions can cause anxiety, especially later in life, is if we experienced neglect or abuse when we were younger. Abuse and neglect can fall under the umbrella of both traumatic life experiences as well as environmental anxiety factors, but these types of ongoing situations can cause an individual to feel and experience anxiety disorders far into the future. At the root of most neglectful and abusive experiences, the victim is left feeling emotionally helpless and damaged. Anxiety, along with a host of other emotional responses, will result from this type of environmental condition. When people who experience neglect and abuse develop anxiety from these experiences, anxiety can become a sort of byproduct of the type of response that this individual will have regarding other situations that life throws at them.

Guided Meditation for Beginners

In addition to neglect and abuse, traumatic experiences of all types can leave a person feeling emotionally helpless and anxious. Some of the signs of emotional anxiety include the following:

### Sign #1: Feeling Like Your Mind's a Blank Slate

The inability to think at all is one sign of emotional anxiety. If you have ever experienced a situation where you cannot seem to recall anything when you need to, this is an example of emotional anxiety at work. By thinking about nothing, your brain is trying to shield itself from the pain that it's likely experienced in the past due to an emotionally trying experience. Not being able to concentrate is another way that emotional anxiety presents itself in people.

### Sign #2: Expecting the Worst

A general feeling of pessimism is another sign that you have experienced some type of emotional trauma in the past. It may be that you are always expecting the worst to happen because your brain is preparing itself in case the worst occurs. In addition to always being on the lookout for the worst to happen, you may also approach situations with dread or extreme apprehension in your head.

### Sign #3: Irritability

If you do not consider yourself an irritable person, yet often find yourself becoming irritated with situations or with the people around you, then you have experienced irritability stemming from emotional anxiety. Irritability often comes from a place where a person feels uncomfortable because he or she cannot control a situation. Control is a key reason why people often experience emotional anxiety, because they are afraid of being hurt, abused, or emotionally neglected like they were in the past.

## Social Anxiety

The last primary cause of anxiety that we're going to look at is social anxiety. Social anxiety can be best defined as a fear that presents itself when you are in social situations. Some key signs of a social anxiety disorder include the following symptoms:

1. **Trouble talking to others:** People with social anxiety disorders often will not be able to talk to new people. They might freeze up, or seem incredibly awkward when presented with the opportunity to make new friends.

2. **Trouble in going to new social events:** Another key sign of a social anxiety disorder is when a person psyches themselves out of attending a social gathering with a group of people they have never met before or know little about. Rather than looking at this situation as an opportunity to meet new people and grow their social circle, someone with social anxiety will feel nothing but dread about the social situation. Many times, this will result in the person avoiding the social gathering at all costs.

The 2 signs above are the most common signs of a social anxiety disorder. Physical body signs that a person suffers from social anxiety include the following:

1. Trouble speaking to the point that no words come out
2. A trembling or shaking in the limbs while in social circles
3. Blushing, even when there is nothing to be embarrassed about

Similar to emotional anxiety that can alter how a person interacts with someone else, social anxiety typically comes from a situation where the person experienced social trauma in the past. For this reason, their brain and body are on high alert and often eager to distance themselves from social situations because of the humiliation or problems that social settings have presented in the past.

## Your Lifestyle Can Cause Anxiety

Lastly, your lifestyle can play a larger role than you may think when it comes to how much anxiety you experience daily. One of the most prevalent ways that anxiety can differ between people with different lifestyles revolves around how often they exercise. People who exercise more frequently are far less likely to experience high levels of stress. On the other hand, people who rarely work out will often have a more difficult time dealing with their anxiety. When you think about our bodies as being able to store energy, it's easy to see how unused energy can cause an individual to overthink or build up in an unhealthy manner. When your mind is tired, it has less time to worry.

In addition to living an active lifestyle, eating unhealthily and drug and alcohol use can cause a person to feel more angst and stress. Caffeine also plays a role in heightening feelings related to anxiety. It's important to note that while eating unhealthy food on its own may not directly lead to stress, the feelings that often accompany unhealthy eating can certainly make a person feel anxious. For example, many people feel stress regarding their physical figure or feelings of lethargy after finishing an unhealthy meal. In extreme situations, anxiety related to a person's lifestyle can even cause this person to become anorexic or engage in illicit drug use frequently.

## The 6 Anxiety Disorders

Anxiety generally grows when someone faces something that is out of their comfort zone and can, therefore, be a lot of difficult circumstances. For instance, if you were going to pass an exam, go to an interview, or offer a lecture. It impacts individuals in distinct respects because, for some, these circumstances can be deemed ordinary, but for many others, they can impact your whole life, such as being unable to sleep, making errors at your job, or being unable to eat correctly. In particular, anxiety occurs when the response is excessive with what is generally anticipated. Anxiety disorders can be categorized into more particular kinds of disorders. Below are the most prevalent types of anxiety.

## Agoraphobia / Panic Disorder

A lot of this is trained conduct. For instance, when you are driving, you encounter a panic attack, and riding can cause your anxiety from this stage forward. It's very feasible that the 2 of them have nothing to do with each other, but the link has been integrated into your brain.

Agoraphobia or adult separation anxiety is a fear of being powerless and alone in the perception of internal risk. This is often articulated as fear of dying, going mad, or losing control of one's conduct. Agoraphobia may contribute to patients staying close to familiar locations and individuals. It could degenerate to the extent of not leaving home.

## Specific Phobia

Specific Phobia is a type of situational anxiety, such as fear of flight, fear of heights, fear of insects or snakes, or claustrophobia. It's not just an act of fear; it's a real fear that manifests itself in anxiety or panic. Specific or single physicians are situationally linked and can be healed by separating themselves from a case or condition that causes anxiety. However, what at first appears to be specific phobias are, at the root, manifestations of agoraphobia that appear to be various phobias. In other words, you may be suffering from agoraphobia if there are a few activities that make you panic or worry.

## Social Phobia

Social Phobia is pathological anxiety manifested specifically as a fear of embarrassment, which may be restricted to public speaking or may be composed of a worldwide shyness that confines social interactions, including dating, marriage, and relationships. People with a personal phobia often have poor self-esteem and think that they are not nice enough. These can be kids who have been picked up or who have overprotective relatives. While agoraphobic individuals are scared to be alone, individuals who have personal phobia often tend to be alone.

### Generalized Anxiety Disorder

General Anxiety Disorder (GAD) is a sheer concern! General anxiety involves times of severe anxiety and stress. The combined impacts of GAD over time on the body. People who have a nervous breakdown or a middle-age crisis often suffer from long-term GAD. In general, GAD does not arrive with panic attacks, phobias, or pathological timidity. It's the basis of all anxiety disorders, but it doesn't imply you're going to have any of the other diseases. Someone who always seems strained, or is always worried, may suffer from overall anxiety.

### Obsessive-Compulsive Disorder

This form of anxiety is generally described by obsessions which are unwanted and intrusive ideas, generally of a brutal or sexual nature. People with obsessive-compulsive disorder (OCD) are trying to rid themselves of these hateful ideas. Short-Term relief from OCD-induced anxiety can be accomplished by participating in compulsions, or ritual senseless behaviors such as saying a phrase over and over, or behavior such as hand washing, inspecting something or going in a certain manner. People with OCD think that their ideas may harm themselves or others. It's not accurate; the ideas are just that, the ideas.

### Post-traumatic Stress Disorder

Post-traumatic stress disorder is an anxiety associated with a very stressful or life-changing scenario that someone has just passed through. Some instances may be, whether they are engaged in brutal crime, conflict or fighting, the murder of a loved one, or in a horrible incident. PTSD includes flashbacks that seem so genuine that an individual may think they're experiencing the incident again. Avoidance is an instrument for individuals who have PTSD. For instance, an individual who has been engaged in a plane accident but has survived may avoid flights and aircraft completely.

# Chapter 2: YOUR BONUS

## BOOK – MEDITATION FOR ANXIETY

## MUSIC- BEST MEDITATION MUSIC

### FREE BOOKS SENT WEEKLY

### JOIN YOUBOOKS EDITIONS READERS BOOK CLUB

get exclusive access to the latest kindle e-book in self help, spirituality and more

Here your TWO SPECIAL FREE GIFTS-SCAN QR CODE

# Chapter 3: What Is Meditation?

Meditation refers to the approach used to train the mind, similar to a fitness program that is used to train the body. It is an ancient practice, which helps us to control our minds, and ultimately our lives to discover ourselves.

You could say that meditation is a way of recharging your batteries and a means to calm down your mind. In many instances, our minds are taken over, which hinders us from having stable thoughts. Through meditation, we can feel and control our thoughts without losing sleep or using so much energy. It is through meditation that we can control our thoughts and minds, and turn off our minds from what we do not need to feel or think about anymore.

Meditation is a strategy that is key to living and feeling well to achieve a happy life. It helps in the elimination of worries, bad thoughts, anxiety, and any other factors that may hinder us from being happy. If carried out regularly, meditation helps in the mitigation of anxiety and stress.

# Benefits of Meditation

When talking about mindfulness pops up, a lot of humans will still try to think that meditation is the sphere of free spirits who have fun out on a woven grass mat somewhere. There is the fact that you should know, and the truth is, there is nothing woo-woo in connection with mindfulness and consciousness meditation. These life occurrences have always been there ever since, and nearly every divine path assimilates approximately form of them. There are interesting facts that you should know about meditation, as discussed below.

### 1. Meditation Will Make You Feel Happy

A lot of people who usually meditate will all the time have a happy life, unlike those who don't. meditation generally has been able to increase the flow of productive thoughts and positive feelings. When you take a few moments meditating most of the time, it can make a huge difference in your life. It has been proven scientifically that meditation brings happiness. A study was done on a group of Buddhist monks when they were meditating to prove this claim. The pre-frontal cortex of the monk's mind was seen to be more active.

### 2. Meditation Will Assist You to Control Nervousness, Despair, and Strain

The enhancement potential of meditation should never be underestimated. A study that has been conducted at the University of Wisconsin showed that meditation would bring psychological effects to the mind. For instance, the researchers found out that the mind controls stress and anxiety shrink when meditation is practiced constantly. When you focus on moment-by-moment knowledge, meditators are trying to teach the brain to be calm, even when going through stressful moments. Due to this, you will also experience knowingly reduced anxiety because of not being sure of what will come along in the future.

### 3. You Shouldn't Be a Religious Leader for You to Meditate

Mind work meditation app organizers have a belief that meditation is probably there to benefit anyone without being bias. Meditation is beyond doctrine, and it is about creating calmness, learning how to be aware, and decluttering the brain. Contemplation has been a vital component in most world religions. You are not supposed to be a religious person for you to meditate. Such news is the best for 1 in 5 Americans who see themselves as spiritual but not religious. Pew Research Centre in January published their findings that told us how the mainstream mindfulness meditation had been recognized in the US despite religious connection.

### 4. Benefits of Meditation Are Immediate

A lot of several health impacts that come about due to meditation are the reasons why so many people opt or think of trying the meditation practice. Some of their benefits can begin making their effects felt fast immediately you begin sitting. The sense of being calm, and having peace of mind are the communal experiences, despite the feeling being fleet and elusive. There is an article that was published in Forbes online, and attorney Jeena Cho listed 6 scientific benefits that had been proven and that you should expect, including a decrease in unspoken race and age prejudice. Other people also argue that meditation is making them have opposite effects, and this is because their minds are getting busier than ever. You are advised to stick with it and try to make your sessions to be short. Meditation is not all about wiping the slate of your brain clean, but it is about being knowledgeable of what is seen. This will make you step ahead, and you will have noticed how busy your brain can be.

### 5. Meditation Will Make You Sleep Easily

Insomnia is a trying, difficult, and troubling disorder. Most humans always talk about having sleepless nights. You should note that almost a third of the

Guided Meditation for Beginners

American population has been suffering due to some form of sleep deficiency, and this can be irregular or long-lasting. You may be among those people who spend their time staring at the ceiling trying to count sheep the whole night, but to no avail, then with such experiences, the best solution is meditation. There is an article in the Harvard Health Blog that authorizes that meditation will trigger a relaxation reply. Due to this, most people will tend to have the opposite problem and will fall to sleep immediately; they start to meditate.

## 6. Meditation Will Give You a Sharp Memory

Having assisted you in being happy and improving your wellbeing, meditation will still assist your memory to be sharp, and your concentration will remain to be steady. When you have mindful meditation, you can train in the remaining conscious of the present moment in an easygoing method. Subsequently, interruptions are less and less likely to carry you away. This is a reason why you should try to meditate.

## 7. Meditation Will Make You Generate Kindness

Other kinds of meditation will increase positive feelings and actions toward yourself and other people. There is a type of mediation called the Metta that is also referred to as loving-kindness meditation. It always starts by improving your kind thoughts and feelings to yourself. When you practice, you will be able to learn about extending kindness and forgiveness to other people. It will be to your friends, acquaintances, and your enemies too. There have been several studies about this kind of meditation demonstrating its capability to have additional peoples' kindness to themselves and other people.

A study done on adults erratically dispensed to a program that had the inclusion of love and kindness meditation found that these reimbursements were dose-dependent. In short, when many people are putting their effort towards Metta meditation, the more positive feelings they will go through. Another research also shows that the positive feelings that you will build through Metta meditation will enhance social anxiety, decrease marriage violence, and assist in controlling anger. You can't imagine that there are people who still want to be convinced even after going through the meditation facts above.

# Forms of Meditation

### Mindfulness Meditation

This is the practice of being present fully—that is not focusing on the past or future. This is the art of being contemporaneous and being present with your thoughts. This means we ought to be aware and not reactive—that is to observe what we do and where we are and not react to what is going on around us. This is in essence, mindfulness. Mindful meditation can usually be practiced anywhere. However, most people prefer to sit with their eyes closed while focusing on their breathing. If you so wish, however, you can be mindful as you walk, drink a cup of tea, work, or relax. When practicing this, one observes their emotions and thoughts from a non-judgmental point of view.

### Guided Meditation

This type of meditation involves visualization and imagery in which one visualizes an object or image of either shape, color, a saintly person, a god, or a goddess, or even a place that makes you feel relaxed. This meditation is referred to as 'guided' as you have a teacher or guide that leads the process. To induce calmness in your space, it is advisable to use as many senses as possible: sight, hearing, touch, smell, and taste.

### Transcendental Meditation

This type of meditation is practiced twice a day for 20 minutes in each session. Its goal is to achieve inner peace without effort or concentration by allowing you to settle inwards to an intense state of relaxation.

## *Vipassana* Meditation

The essence of *Vipassana* is self-transformation through self-observation. This phenomenon is accomplished by observing different sensations on the physical aspect of the body to forge a strong connection between mind and body. This connection generates a balanced mind full of love and compassion.

Vipassana in this tradition is taught over a 10-day course where students are expected to observe a set of 5 precepts throughout the course including abstaining from lies, stealing, intoxicants, sexual activity, and killing any species.

## *Metta* Meditation

This is also known as loving-kindness meditation as it is the practice of sharing one's merits and directing well wishes of happiness, peace, and harmony to others. It is a practice that happens after *Vipassana* and mindful meditations.

The usual practice happens when one is in a calm and relaxed state and after a few breaths, one will slowly and steadily repeat words of good wishes of happiness, peace, and harmony to oneself and then later directing it to other people they may wish and visualize. The mediation usually ends with the universal mantra "May All Beings Be Happy."

## Chakra Meditation

The spiritual power and energy centers present in the human body are chakras. There are 7 chakras in total, and they are all located at different points in the body: third eye chakra, crown chakra, the throat chakra, the navel chakra, the heart chakra, the sacral chakra, and the root chakra. The practice, therefore, involves bringing oneness by unblocking the chakras.

The use of crystals and incense is very common in this practice as it helps in concentrating on the different chakras present. Sometimes, visualizing a color and its corresponding chakra while meditating is another common technique. Yes, chakras do have colors.

### Yoga Meditation

Known to be one of the most popular forms of meditation, yoga gets its roots in ancient India. There are 8 known types of yoga: *Vinyasa, Iyengar, Power, Bikram, Jivamukti, Ashtanga, Sivananda,* and *Yin* yoga. All these types have the characteristic of breathing exercises while trying to achieve different postures. The practice promotes calmness and flexibility.

Due to the different types of techniques available, it is advisable to do ample research and find whichever type suits you, depending on any type of physical ailment that might come in the way.

# Chapter 4: Getting Started

## How to Meditate

Meditation is a great—and logically demonstrated—habit for a solid body and mind. Be that as it may, a few people battle with the time, consistency, center, and system required to get meditation right.

What many people don't know is, you don't need to take a seat and close your eyes for a considerable length of time a day—because there are other far less demanding approaches to get your psyche into a thoughtful state, and appreciate the advantages of this ancient practice.

For example:

### 1. While you walk your dog

As you're strolling Jack, instead of meditating on the large number of things you're stalling on, take a stab at giving careful attention to your environment.

- Recognize the sounds, the general population, the climate. What do you smell? What would you be able to see? What would you be able to hear out yonder? How does your body feel?

By taking a careful walk, you're discharging endorphins, which enable you to build your joy level, and even diminish stress and live longer.

### 2. While you make coffee or tea

Begin your morning with more profound concentration, lucidity, and peace by rehearsing this simple reflective custom.

- As you make your tea or coffee, concentrate your attention on your developments.
- Close your eyes and notice the tea, taste, enjoy it. Furthermore, as you experience the ritual custom, be deliberately mindful of your breath.

You can likewise apply this while you cook your most loved supper or heat.

### 3. While you do the dishes

Doing dishes or clearing your floor doesn't need to be an errand. This is the ideal time for you to associate with yourself and feel grounded.

### 4. While you shower

Guided Meditation for Beginners

Have you at any point asked why your best thoughts tend to come while you're showering?

The shower is where we can develop mindfulness. When we get tranquil, when we get still, when we rest, you could state, in mindfulness, our natural drive to see associations that we didn't see the prior minute is unobstructed.

On the off chance that you need to take it somewhat further, as you shower, you can even envision accomplishing your objectives and the feeling that will wash over you as you do.

5.  **While you tune in to your main tune**

- Practicing mindfulness or meditation can be as straightforward as tuning in to your main song—insofar as you're centered around your breathing and the feeling that the song brings out in you.

6.  **While you ride the transport or sit in your auto**

- Sit serenely. Take long and full breaths. Recognize the warm sun stroking your face. Welcome the delightful city lights or scene. Also, let your mind take you all alone trip.

As you now know, the benefits of meditation can be conveyed into the most ordinary exercises—helping you acknowledge life all the more, inhabit a slower pace, embrace new propensities, and be more joyful.

# Practical Advice on Meditation

### To What Extent Should I Meditate?

If you are new to meditation, I suggest beginning gradually. Begin with only 5 minutes every day. Bit by bit increment the time more than half a month.

When I began reflecting, 5 minutes felt like an unfathomable length of time. I now practice for 30 minutes every day, and here and there I am astonished at how rapidly it passes!

### Where Should I Meditate?

Locate a comfortable spot where you can sit. You can sit on the floor (utilizing a pad or pad for help if necessary) or sit upright in a seat, with your feet laying on the floor.

A few people suggest that you don't rest on your back, however, I figure you ought to think in whatever stance works for you (unless resting influences you to fall asleep!)

You can meditate anyplace, yet I like having an extraordinary place in my home for my training.

### What Do I Do?

The least demanding meditation strategy is to count the breath. I forget about each in-breath and breath with a similar number. So my mind concentrates on "One" (in-breath), "One" (out-breath), "Two" (in-breath), "Two" (out-breath), etc. When I hit 10 (which seldom occurs before my mind has wandered!) I begin once again at one. On the off chance that you don't care for counting, you can essentially rehash to yourself "in, out... in, out..."

At the point when your mind wanders, which it will do (that's what the mind does!) tenderly guide your attention back to your breath. On the off chance that you have to begin once again counting because you don't recollect the latest relevant point of interest, that is fine! The key is to not reprimand or judge yourself for giving your attention a chance to wander. Actually... seeing that your psyche has wandered is the general purpose of meditation you are winding up more mindful of the activities of your mind!

Indeed, even the moderately basic guideline to "take after the breath" can sound somewhat obscure or confounding. A supportive method is to bring your attention where you most notice the vibe of the breath—in the chest and lungs? The nose? The stomach? That is your stay. Each time your mind wanders, return to the physical vibes of relaxing.

At the point when thought emerges, it's anything but difficult to get diverted and tail them and draw in them and explain them and investigate them... An accommodating practice is to just name the contemplations: "stressing," "arranging," "recollecting." Don't stress over making sense of the exact mark for the kind of thought you're having. Simply "considering" will do, as well!

What's more, if the thoughts don't leave? It's still alright. I adore that depiction of the training.

### How Do I Fit This Into My Day?

The critical thing is to make it a propensity. After numerous long stretches of reliable practice, it will end up being a vital piece of your day, such as brushing your teeth!

Changing your habits over some time makes new neural systems in your mind, and the training will turn out to be a piece of your day-by-day schedule.

## Knocks Along the Road

- In any case, nothing's happening!: Meditation is about non-judgmental mindfulness. We have to not bring desires into our practice. You may encounter a snapshot of significant understanding amid a meditation session. Or, then again you may be truly exhausted. You may feel fretful and disturbed. Or, on the other hand, you may feel quiet and relaxed.
- Meditation is tied in with grasping whatever is right now: The

advantages of meditation—more noteworthy mindfulness and discretion, increased calm and empathy—will rise after some time. In any case, every individual session will be unique. So in case you're exhausted, simply take note of, "This is the thing that fatigue feels like." If you're content, take note of, "This is the thing that satisfaction feels like."

- Meditating for 10 minutes daily is limitlessly superior to meditating for 70 minutes once per week: Attempt to meditate oftentimes (consistently if conceivable), regardless of the possibility that that just means sitting for a couple of minutes.

- Start little: If you endeavor to meditate for 30 minutes right from the beginning, I can practically ensure that you will get disappointed and disheartened. I prescribe beginning with five minutes, and just increase that time when you're comfortable. Regardless of the possibility that you sit for 5 minutes, and you find that your mind wanders the entire time, you will in any case get unfathomable advantages from meditation.

- Pick a gentle alarm: On the off chance that your clock is uproarious and jolting, reckoning the caution will occupy your attention amid meditation.

- Meditate in a peaceful place: Having fewer distractions around you will normally enable you to meditate better, and will make your meditation significantly more profitable.

- It's most straightforward to lose your attention amid your out-breath: Your in-breath is exceptionally articulated and simple to focus on, and the vast majority's mind wanders on their out-breaths (me included). This merits remembering.

- Be understanding with yourself when your mind wanders It is very easy to end up disappointed with yourself when your mind wanders, yet don't. Your meditations will be substantially more gainful when you delicately bring your mind back.

# Chapter 5: Dealing With Stress

To properly manage your specific stressors, you must know what exactly causes your stress in the first place. Some people have a higher stress tolerance compared to others, but people often share the same causes of stress, just like back in ancient days, when most people shared the same stressor of being hunted by a stronger predator, like a bear. Nowadays, people likely share the same stressor of not being able to financially support themselves and ending up in an impoverished situation. When a person can identify which situations are causing their stress, they can then learn how to either manage those stressors or prevent them in the first place. In this chapter, we will be learning about external and internal stress factors, the common causes of stress, common triggers of stress, and the importance of understanding what your stress triggers are. Let's dive right in.

## External and Internal Stress Factors

To effectively manage one's stress, it begins with being able to identify what your sources of stress are and then developing the proper strategies to manage them. An effective way to do this is to simply make a list of challenges, concerns, or situations that triggers your stress response. If you can think of a few of these situations immediately, take a moment to write them down to identify what your top issues are right now. You may notice that some of your stressors are events that happen to you outside your control or while others seem to happen within yourself. Let's take a look at external factors first.

### External Stress Factors

Keep in mind that external stress factors are situations or events that happen to you. Most of the time, these situations are out of your control unless you take active measures to prevent them. External factors include:

- **Social:** Relationships tend to be a huge source of stress for most people. This could range from meeting new people to going on a blind date or even just having a night out with your friends. When you are in a relationship or close contact with your family, stress tends to spawn from those places. Think about the last fight you had with your significant other, how stressed did you feel?
- **Workplace:** Workplaces tend to be a huge source of stress for many people. Common stressors within the workplace include; sales targets, urgent deadlines, a demanding boss, endless emails, and an impossible workload. Toxic work environments make it very hard for people to not take their work home with them.
- **Unpredictable events:** Events that happen out of the blue like getting into a fender bender or your basement flooding during a storm can cause you to have high levels of stress. These are events that are hard to prevent but unfortunately happens to all of us.
- **Environment:** The environment of the world around us can be a big source of stress. Imagine being stuck in traffic for a few hours a day to get to work or having to prepare for an incoming snowstorm. Other factors like sudden noises from animals (barking dogs) can easily influence your stress levels and mood.
- **Major life changes:** Although a lot of life changes can be positive such

as a job promotion, a new home, a planned pregnancy, and a new marriage, some can be negative. Major negative life changes, like a divorce or the death of a loved one, can cause high levels of stress for most people.

There are many strategies that you can use to manage external stress factors. We will learn more of these later on in the book, but common strategies that are effective include; getting enough sleep, being physically active, and eating a healthy diet. Utilizing others for help can also be helpful. Other factors like learning to be assertive, increasing your problem-solving skills, and managing your time more effectively have also been reported as being effective for people that are looking to manage their stress. Like I mentioned earlier, start by writing a list of possible causes of stress. By identifying what those are, you can slowly determine which strategies would be efficient in managing it.

### Internal Stress Factors

Not all stress is caused by external things happening to you. Most people's stress is actually due to internal factors. Feelings and thoughts that pop into your head that cause you to feel stressed are known as internal stress factors. For instance, if there is a deadline at work looming and you begin to have negative thoughts like "I'm going to get fired if I don't finish this on time," then that is an internal stress factor. This is why people who have anxiety disorders tend to feel more stressed frequently because they are constantly having anxious thoughts and a negative pattern of thinking. Having constant negative thoughts causes stress levels to rise. Here are some examples of internal stress factors:

Beliefs: Beliefs can be a person's expectations, opinions, or attitudes, or a combination of all 3. Most people don't think about how their beliefs shape their experiences, but having preset thought processes tends to cause stress with people. For instance, the expectations you have for yourself to advance your career or simply the expectations you have to create the perfect holiday party for your family and friends.

Uncertainty and lack of control: Not many people enjoy not having control or not knowing what's about to happen. This can often cause stress when a person is faced with the fear of the unknown. For instance, think about how you may feel when you're awaiting the test results from a medical check-up.

Fears: Everyone has fears; some people have more than others. Common fears that people have are flying, public speaking, and fear of failure.

The upside to all of this is that people can change and control their thoughts. The downside is, however, that people's fears, expectations, and attitudes have been drilled into their brains for a very long time, and it will often take a lot of time and effort to rewire them.

## Common Causes of Stress

Although stress is a normal human reaction and is one that we need to survive, too much of it can cause us serious harm. Despite stress being something that everyone has experienced and continues to experience, it can manifest and be caused by different things from person to person. For example, one person may become very stressed and overwhelmed when they are stuck in a traffic jam, and they have some other place to be, while another person may be in the same situation but feel indifferent. Some people might be bothered all day if they argued with their significant other while another person may not be bothered by it at all! Some people may already aware of what exactly causes them to feel stressed. However, since preventing and overcoming extreme stress is crucial to having a happy and healthy life, it is worth learning about what factors may be causing you to stress specifically. Just because someone else gets stressed out about certain things, it may not apply to you! By learning specifically about what your stressors are, you can build a stress-reduction plan that is catered to you as an individual.

## How to Overcome Stress

To prevent serious health problems, people must get their stress under control. Although most people think that stress is just a psychological feeling and they can overcome it just by "pushing through" or ignoring it, they are very wrong. Thoughts directly affect a person's brain chemistry, and the effects of stress are very physical. This is why learning to overcome stress is important in maintaining a healthy and balanced life. There are various ways to do it that range from stress prevention to stress management to therapy. We will be focusing on tips that you can use in day-to-day life to help overcome stress. Let's take a look at 8 tips to overcome stress:

Guided Meditation for Beginners

## Tip #1: Identifying Your Stressors

When you are used to dealing with a certain kind of stress, it is easy to overlook the thoughts and feelings that you have about it. You may know that you are always worrying about deadlines at work, but maybe it's your procrastination that is causing your stress, not the job itself. To help you identify your main causes of stress, you must take a close look at your excuses, habits, and attitude:

- Do you normally blame your stress on external events like people or situations? Do you view your stress as "normal" and no different from others?
- Do you think that your stress is a part of your work and personal life? E.g. "Things are always crazy at work" or "I'm just an anxious person!"
- Do you define your stress as "temporary?" E.g. "I'm just super busy right now!" even though you don't remember the last time you weren't stressed?

The first step to overcoming your stress is to accept responsibility for the role that you play in maintaining or creating it. Until then, your stress level won't be something you can control.

## Tip #2: Practice Stress Management

Stress may be an automatic response created by our bodies. Some stressors can come up at very predictable times.

- *Avoid unnecessary stress:* Although it isn't healthy to constantly be avoiding situations that need to be addressed, you can still eliminate a lot of stressors by avoiding them. Here are a few tips:
  - *Learn to say "no."* Know what your boundaries are and stick to them. This is relevant in your personal and professional life. When you take on too many things, you are creating

stress for yourself. Be able to distinguish the difference between your 'musts' and 'shoulds'. Learn to say no when you know you are taking on too much.

- o *Avoid people who cause stress.* If there is a certain someone who tends to cause you stress, either end the relationship or limit how much time you spend with them.
- o *Control your environment.* If watching the news stressed you out, turn it off. If driving in traffic stresses you out, consider a different method of travel. If Christmas shopping at a busy mall is stressful for you, consider doing your shopping online this year.
- o *Minimize your to-do list.* Prioritize the things you really need to do and analyze your current schedule. If you have too many things on the go at the moment, let go of the tasks that aren't 100% necessary.

- *Alter the situation:* If a stressful situation isn't avoidable, try to change it instead. This may involve changing your communication style or how you operate in your everyday life.
  - o *Express your feelings and emotions instead of hiding them.* If something is bothering you, whether it's a situation or it's a person, learn to be assertive and diplomatically communicate your feelings. If you have an upcoming exam that you need to study for and your chatty sister had just gotten home, tell her directly, but nicely, that you only have 5 minutes to chat before you have to get back to studying. If you don't communicate your feelings, stress, and resentment will increase.
  - o Be open to compromise. If you are asking someone to change the way they behave, be open to making some changes yourself too. If both people are willing to take one step back, you'll have a much better shot of finding a happy middle ground.
  - o *Create a balanced schedule.* If you are only working and not

doing leisurely activities, you are setting yourself up for burnout. Try to find the perfect balance between your professional and personal life.

- *Adapt to the stressor:* If you aren't able to change the stressor, change yourself instead. People are adaptable creatures. You can find a way to adapt to situations that are stressful and regain control.
  - o *Look at your problems in a different way.* Try to look at situations that are stressful from a more positive light. For instance, rather than being upset about being stuck in traffic, try to think of it as an opportunity to listen to some music or your favorite podcast.
  - o *Take a step back and look at the big picture.* Try to get some perspective on whatever stressful situation you are feeling at the moment. Ask yourself how important this one stressful situation will be to you in the future. Focus your time and energy on things that will matter in the future.
  - o *Being a perfectionist is a big source of stress.* Change your standards and stop stressing yourself out from holding such high standards. Set more reasonable standards for yourself and learn to be comfortable with who you are.
  - o *Practice gratitude frequently.* When you are feeling extremely stressed out, take some time to think about all the things in your life that you appreciate. This includes materialistic things and your positive qualities. This strategy is simple and helps give people a better perspective.
- *Accept things that can't be changed:* In some cases, stress is unavoidable. For instance, you can't change big stressors like a death of a family member or having a serious illness. In these cases, the best way to cope with your stress is to accept things for the way they are. Although acceptance may be hard at first, it is beneficial in the long run to not fight it so hard.
  - o *Don't try to control things that you can't.* There are tons of things in life that are beyond our control, especially in

regards to other people. Rather than being stressed because of someone else's actions, focus on things that are in your control, such as how you react to stressful situations.

o *Be optimistic.* When you are faced with a big obstacle, try to look at it as an opportunity for growth rather than a setback. If it was your own choices that led you to this stressful circumstance, reflect on those decisions and learn to make better ones in the future.

o *Practice forgiveness.* Accept the fact that nobody is perfect in this world and that everyone will make mistakes. Let go of negative feelings like resentment and anger. Allow yourself to be free from negative energy by forgiving and moving on.

o *Express your feelings.* Expressing the things that you are going through can be challenging. However, a problem shared is a problem halved. Talk to a friend or a loved one for some support.

**Tip #3: Get Active**

Oftentimes, when people are feeling stressed, they likely do not want to get up and do something physical. However, exercising is a great way to relieve stress, you don't have to spend hours at the gym to reap the benefits, you can simply do a light exercise or just go for a quick walk for your brain to release the endorphins that make you feel good. People get the most benefit from exercise if they do it for at least 30 minutes per day. Small exercise activities will add up for a day. Here are some suggestions that you can try to incorporate into your schedule:

- Play an active game with your family/friends (e.g., Ping pong, Wii).
- Find an exercise partner and hold each other accountable.
- Parking your car as far as you can and get yourself to walk to wherever you're going.
- Walk to do your errands instead of driving.

Guided Meditation for Beginners

- If you have a dog, take him/her out for a walk.
- Play some music and dance around.

### Tip #4: Socialize

Spending quality time with other people gives us a sense of calming and makes us feel understood and safe. In-person interactions counteract our body's fight or flight mechanism and are a natural stress reliever. So, make an effort to go out and socialize regularly with family and friends. Keep in mind that the people you choose to hang out with don't need to be able to help with your stress. Simply being a good listener is enough for you to get some weight off of your shoulders. People who care about you will be happy that you are comfortable with opening up to them and will strengthen your relationship with them. Although it's not always realistic to have someone close by that you can talk to about your feelings, building a close circle of friends that you can talk to can improve your resilience to the stresses of life. Here are some relationship building suggestions:

- Talk to your colleagues at work.
- Meet up with a friend for lunch or coffee.
- Help out others by volunteering.
- Call to chat with an old friend.
- Confide in someone you trust like a teacher or your sold sports coach.

### Tip #5: Leisurely Activities

Besides changing your attitudes regarding stressful events, you can lower the stress you feel in everyday life by making sure you are getting enough "me" time. Don't forget about leisurely activities when you're caught up in the busyness of life. Take care of your own needs first. Make time for relaxation and fun events, and you'll be in a much better spot to handle your stress. Here are some things you could do:

- *Practice relaxation:* Take up some relaxation practice through meditation, breathing exercises, or yoga. This helps activate a person's relaxation response and promotes a state of restfulness. As you learn these techniques, you will notice that your stress levels have lowered, and your mind and body will function in a more relaxed manner.
- *Use your sense of humor:* Learn the ability to laugh at yourself and don't take life so seriously. Laughing more often helps fight off stress.
- *Do something that you like every day:* Schedule time for activities that make you happy; this could be playing video games or working on your custom motorcycle.

*Set aside time for leisure:* Make sure to make time for relaxation in your everyday schedule. Don't let other obligations take over your leisurely time. Take a break to recharge, so you can feel energized.

**Tip #6: Time Management**

Guided Meditation for Beginners

When you are bad at managing your time, this can create a lot of stress. This could either be in the form of not having enough time to get the necessities done, or it could be not scheduling enough time for self-care. When a person is stretched too thin, it is hard to stay relaxed and calm. You will also be more likely to cut back on the healthy living activities that you should be doing to better maintain your stress. This includes getting enough sleep or exercising. There are a few things that you can do to achieve a better work-life balance:

- *Delegate responsibility:* You don't have to do everything yourself all the time. Other people can help you with tasks, and they are likely very willing to help! Let go of the idea of needing to control every step of the way. By doing this, you are letting go of unnecessary stress.
- *Break tasks into smaller ones:* One large task seems overwhelming, but breaking it down into manageable steps will lift a lot of stress from your shoulders. Focus on one step at a time, and you'll slowly start to feel a sense of accomplishment that will motivate you into doing more steps.
- *Prioritize your tasks:* Make a list of things you need to do and do them in order of importance. Finish your most important things first, and suddenly you'll feel a lot better.
- *Don't overcommit:* Avoid overscheduling things such as back-to-back engagements or trying to fit too many activities in one day. We often underestimate how long it takes to do something, so if you're overscheduled, you'll likely begin to feel stressed out.

### Tip #7: Maintaining Balance

On top of increasing your activity levels through exercising, make sure you are also eating a healthy diet. Having the proper nutrients helps increase people's resistance to stress. Here are some tips:

- *Get enough sleep:* Adults need 7–9 hours of sleep every night. Getting enough sleep helps keep our minds healthy. Feeling tired and sluggish will only make your stress worse.

- *Limit consumption of alcohol, drugs, or cigarettes:* Self-medicating through the use of drugs or alcohol may provide temporary relief from stress, but it may cause you to become reliant on it. Rather than avoiding the problem, deal with it head-on so that it doesn't re-occur.
- *Reduce the intake of sugar and caffeine:* Although sugar and caffeine may boost your energy for a while, it always ends in a crash in both your energy and your mood. When you reduce your coffee and sugar intake, you will begin to feel more relaxed and be able to get better sleep.

*Eat a healthy diet:* Healthy bodies are much better at dealing with stress, so pay attention to what you're eating. Start your day by eating a healthy breakfast to boost your energy and help you have a clearer mind throughout the day.

### Tip #8: Relieving Stress in the Moment

When you are stressed, the best way to deal with it is not to ignore it. It is to overcome it as it is happening. If you are frustrated by the traffic jam during your morning commute, find a way to manage your stress levels. You can reduce stress the fastest by practicing breathing exercises and mindfulness. Pay attention to the things going on around you such as what you hear, feel, see, and taste. You can listen to relaxing sounds like the flow of a river or ocean waves. Find out what sort of sounds and experiences relax you the most and make sure you have access to it at all times to use it during moments of high stress.

# Chapter 6: 10 Days of Practical Meditation

Sometimes you can look and see hundreds of people sitting in silence with purpose, and nothing is happening except for extreme silence and deep thinking. It is very powerful to experience and witness hundreds of people practicing meditation at one time. It can be very motivating as well as doing something to your spirit that feels natural and great.

In this chapter, we will discuss a 10-day guide on how to practice meditation—and keep practicing it!

## Day 1: Meditating Sitting Down

Sitting down does not just mean being seated. It means taking your seat in a relationship with the present moment, taking your stand in your life while you are sitting. Adopting and keeping a positive posture will give you pride, which will immediately change how you look and feel about yourself. Being aware of your physical sensations and thoughts while you are sitting upright is essential to meditation while you are sitting down. Whatever emotion you may have, let it flow right through you, and do not let it consume you.

We can do this anytime, in any way, just make your mind aware of it and decide you want to do it. It takes many hours of practice, and you will just want to make sure that you are comfortable and relaxed.

Having strength and stability can come from sitting directly on the floor and crossing your legs as you do your meditating. You can also use a large pillow or cushion, which will assist in raising your butt off the floor to a more aligned level.

This is more about being able to concentrate and focusing on keeping your mind sitting still. Just as in meditating while lying down, establish your posture, let yourself go, and allow the present moment to take charge, then awareness is immediate.

Focus on the sensations of your breath in the places of the body where they are most popular to you. Your nose and your stomach are great places to focus on to practice awareness of each breath.

Focus on the feeling of each breath as it passes through your nostrils and makes your stomach rise in and out up and down. Our minds will always wander away from our primary focus to go into something it feels is more entertaining.

This will continue to happen regularly because we are human, so we can just remember to acknowledge it and remind our minds to refocus on what is important at that moment in time.

Get your mind back on the thought of your breathing and begin to expand your awareness to include sensations within the body. Whatever it is that you are feeling, be aware of that, and own it. If you feel pain in your knee, let it be known that there is a pain in that knee, the key here is to be aware of it, so that you can move on from it.

You do not have to be consumed or held as a prisoner by it. Just sit with an awareness of those sensations, acknowledge them as pleasant or unpleasant, realizing that is exactly what you are experiencing at that moment. The breath and the body come together as a complete being at this moment, and they are seen and felt like one.

You can imagine all your thoughts and emotions like the ocean flowing peacefully and calmly. Whether you are meditating or not, it can be helpful to look at this as an excuse to sit by and take in the beautiful sounds of the ocean as we stare at the wonderfully inspiring beach.

All the time, we are present in each moment and make sure to welcome the presence of awareness to be infinite like the birds that fly in the sky. As stated before, it will take much dedication and practice to master this, but you will benefit along the way from all of your work.

## Day 2: Meditating While Standing

You can meditate while standing up the same way that you can meditate while sitting, lying down, or walking. It is 1 of the 4 popular ways in which people all over the world are now practicing their meditation.

When you think of standing meditation, it can be helpful for you to think about a tree. I know that sounds kind of silly, but the logic is that a tree has all the knowledge and discipline that it needs to be able to stand in one place for a very long time.

Yet trees have managed to remain in a very timeless state and are still present and at the moment with us, no matter what their age seems to be. It may help your understanding of this if you go and stand next to your favorite type of tree for a while.

Try to listen and imagine hearing exactly what the tree would be hearing at that moment. You are to try to become an immediate family with the tree so that you can understand the language in which it is communicating with the universe.

You can physically experience what the tree feels by standing barefoot on the ground and becoming one with the soil. As you share the energy of tree, soil, and universe, you will begin to feel a very natural and free type of feeling in your spirit.

The same way that it is with other types of meditation, it can help if you keep up the practice for a longer time than you feel like doing it. When you get that very first impulse to quit, that is when you want to focus, dig deep and keep going.

That will serve as a very vital test of your commitment, self-control, and determination. It is not easy to accomplish at first, but you will be able to do it if you just push yourself beyond each comfort zone that you try and hold onto.

Stay consistent and do not stop trying, when you can imagine yourself being completely inside your body, without feeling the ground touching your feet, and the sensation of your head being elevated with a sense of grace and ease looking into the direction of the Highest who is watching us all from the heavens.

Being consciously embedded in the current state of your own life and realizing that it is vital and important that you assume and retain control of your life and the direction in which it is going.

How you stand, the way that you should hold your hands, and the posture in which you need to hold your arms are all essential to this practice. Your arms should be relaxed while hanging directly along each side of your body. This stance should be held for a few moments as the awareness is claimed and stood in.

You want to be sure that you align yourself and be as centered as possible because you are going to stand strong, tall, and with much dignity. Now you can surrender yourself into just simply being with what is.

Anyone can practice standing meditation anywhere, at any time, whenever they may feel like they are ready to give it a try. Some people have tried meditation, found it too difficult or boring, or just did not understand the point of it all.

We would like to welcome back those who are willing to give it another try and who are looking to make a positive change in their lives. This can be practiced anytime you think about doing it. It can be while you are waiting on the elevators, while you are driving, while you are waiting on the bus or train, it is all in your mind.

### Meditating While Walking

With walking, we have experienced our bodies a little differently than when we are sitting or lying down during meditation. Bringing our attention to our feet and using that contact between each of our feet and the ground, we can imagine it as if we are giving kisses to the world each time we step down.

When the mind wanders off while we are walking and meditating, it is no different from it is with any other meditation practice. As long as we take note of where it went and get it back into the moment, we can continue the harmony with our breathing and our steps. Take slow strides when you are walking, and you will notice more about nature and things around you.

Walking meditation can be done at different speeds because, the same way life can throw us in another direction, our minds will assist us with the transition from mindful walking into mindful running, and that can be a very helpful tool in the practice of meditation.

You can begin by standing still, bringing awareness to your body as a whole, and realize those impulses in the mind that are going to initiate the process of walking by lifting one foot, so we become aware of each time we lift each foot.

Now you will get the actual impulse to finally take that first step forward, which will now begin to bring us into touch with the full aspect of each sensation that we experience in our bodies that are connected with walking, lifting the heel of the foot, and the actual swinging of your leg as it is being moved forward.

Coordinating all this with our breathing while being able to observe each breath as our body moves is essential to mastering this practice. While being mindful, a useful way to coordinate this is that you can breathe in like the back of your heel raises off of the ground and breathe out each time it touches down.

Now I want you to think of what you are going to be doing with your hands during this time. You just need to be aware of the fact that they are hanging down on the side of your body and let them rest right where they are.

There is never just one specific way to accomplish these practices. You can experiment with what feels right for you and the way that you live. There is no right or wrong way; it is all about practicing, being consistent, and finding what is comfortable for you while you are walking.

## Day 3: Meditating While Lying Down

The most challenging thing to do when you are trying to practice lying down while you meditate is staying awake. This takes more work than the actual meditation because as soon as you get relaxed, you begin to get sleepy. You have to remember not to fall asleep because you can get so relaxed that you can fall right into drowsiness, unawareness and be out for the count before you realize it.

And without practice this happens quite a bit, most people have talked about how hard it is to stay awake during this process, and without practice, you are going to fall into drowsiness, get sleepier, and the deeper the sense of relaxation, you are asleep.

Meditating while lying down, has different types of benefits. During the early stages of meditation practice, it can be more comfortable for some people. As you concentrate on your breathing, it gets easier to feel the gravity. You can, at times, feel as if you are floating, and that can bring about an extreme amount of peace.

Practicing mindfulness while you lay on your back is called Yoga by many people.

Place a padded surface like a rug, a large cushion, or even a mattress that you may have on the floor.

You can simply dedicate your focus to being on hearing, bringing back your attention to hearing over and over again when it wanders off. Just bring it back. It's a powerful way to practice coming to your senses through the sense of hearing.

Some people find it very relaxing to meditate with their eyes closed while they lay down and have stated that it helps retain awareness and easier to become focused and concentrate.

It can be very valuable if you can practice meditating while you are lying down before you fall asleep, and again as soon as you wake up. This can affect how you choose to go about your day and will determine the true intention before you even get out of bed.

You can decide that you are going to have a great day, and you will not get caught in the negativity of any circumstance or situation. That is a positive practice that you can do daily to help ensure that you have a good day.

You can do the same thing when you lay in bed at the end of the night before you go to sleep. Experience your body and your mind. Think about what happened during the craziness of your day and be aware of each of the senses you have. Plan out how you intend to relax and be at peace during your sleep, enjoy and remember your dreams.

Anytime you are laying down is a chance to work at getting stronger at this. There are constantly new possibilities for learning and growing and healing. And without realizing it once again, there are opportunities many times throughout the day that we can take a few moments to lay down and practice our mindfulness and meditation techniques.

Our bodies need rehabilitation and to learn how to live again. Sometimes this can be after we suffer an injury or an illness, and our body just needs some positive, healthy attention because it has been neglected. You can take the time to get it back to where it needs to be, paying close attention and feeling your body movement by movement sense by sense as you go through your day.

That goes back to what we said earlier about paying close attention to your body, and it will tell you exactly what it needs, and you will be able to act accordingly. We never know to the degree to which our bodies are responding to us, but they definitely will respond.

The body loves the process of getting all of this new attention, care, compassion, and love. It receives all of that and will return it to you with the same amount of love.

# Day 4: Yoga a Great Gift

The more you do a profound meditation practice, especially when you do it openly and honestly, the more you will develop your strength, balance, and flexibility of the mind. Learning how to focus on the practice of deep healing and all the complexities of the body, in general, goes hand in hand with the practice and powerful use of mindful yoga.

It is said that in *Hatha* yoga, there are over 84.000 popular postures and positions, and breathing is an essential part of the yoga experience.

How we breathe while moving between each maintaining posture becomes very important, and the level of our awareness of our breathing and senses is dependent upon this.

The actual postures themselves are not what the vital key is here, your attitude that you will bring to the practice is what is extremely important to the process of being mindful and meditating.

The process of yoga in the West is described as a strong desire to move forward to gaining a greater consciousness of the mind and body. While also being committed to true well-being and healthy lives for people all over the world.

Mindfulness and stress reduction practices have always included *Hatha* yoga, which has relied on the medical arena because they refer to it as being known to reverse heart disease and be very useful in the reduction of cancer cells.

Yoga can be practiced very gently and slowly. You want to start slowly but effectively, so get your body used to postures that you do not usually put yourself into. This will help your body get used to and welcome new postures and positions.

Over some time of doing this, it will result in an increase in range of motion in all of your joints and open up areas of movement in your body that will assist in the improvement of your strength and balance.

We have talked about the parts of practicing your meditation while you are sitting down or lying down and how you have to do this regularly; it is the same way with practicing yoga. You need to be consistent. It is going to start to serve your body and spirit like a daily vitamin and mineral that you need to sustain good overall health.

You have to get your body used to the constant stretches and postures daily, so this must be practiced continually. It feels so great getting your body down on the floor and getting it ready for stretching and different postures.

Being open and fully aware that you are getting ready to explore and stretch the limits and capabilities of how your body is used to being able to maneuver.

Over a long time, once you start to practice this, and you are consistent with it, you are going to notice that your body is changing right before your eyes, and it feels great. This result is usually the same no matter how old you are or what kind of condition your body is in.

The secret is to be aware of your own body, know your limits, and take it slow. You will be excited and even more motivated when you start to witness the flexibility and strength that your body has now.

There is no more straining or over-stretching of the muscles because you have learned appropriate posture and correct stretching techniques during this time. And still, you are in the learning process, trying to move forward and trying to continue to motivate yourself.

The focus should be on getting your energy in the right place because we all know there is always something that will come along and distract you or completely turn you off from working towards your goals.

Guided Meditation for Beginners

We cannot allow that to happen, at least not permanently. It is not over until the very end, and when you learn how to really and truly pay attention to your body, it will teach you what you need to know about it.

That's why it is extremely important to be mindful and aware of your body; it is the only one that you get. It gets stronger and healthier over time, the more you pay attention to it and listen to it.

Be sure to be mindful, meditate, eat right and exercise, and the state of your mental and physical health will be great!! Also, through the practice of mindful yoga, you will be able to get a deep sense of what it means to inhabit the body and develop a richer sense of living in the body at the moment. Some refer to it as learning to live again.

## Day 5: Growth in Yoga Practice

Yoga is a modern practice that more and more people from all walks of life have started to take advantage of, and the awareness of the health benefits has become huge. Flexibility, health, and emotional reasons have all been listed as the reasons for so many new people getting into yoga.

There have been many studies done, and as of November 2018, we can see that, in the United States alone, the number of people who are practicing yoga has grown by over 50% in the last 4 years to over 36 million in 2018.

In 2008 only 15.8 million people were participating in yoga in the United States, in 2012 there were approximately 20.4 million, and finally, in 2018, there were around 36 million people practicing yoga.

Many people have stated that they are into the way that it makes them feel afterward, it seems to make most feel great. Some have even stated that the pain they were feeling was reduced after practicing yoga and that each time they do it, they feel better and better.

Many people believe that yoga is a spiritual gift from God that was made to heal your body naturally. It has been known to enhance health and act as a preventative measure against aging, disease, stress, and depression.

Yoga can motivate you to want to live a much healthier lifestyle because your body will begin to feel so much different that you will have to make a change if you listen to it. When you are physically active, it goes hand in hand with the practice of yoga.

Many studies have shown that people who practice yoga live a longer and healthier life. Most people who do yoga have also changed the way they eat, as well as becoming more active if they were not already.

In Japan, the number of people doing yoga in 2005 was 295,000, and by 2010, there were 1.2 million people. This represents a 413% increase in just 5 years.

There are multiple benefits of yoga, and people practice and enjoy it for many reasons, including just to feel better physically. Multiple studies have been conducted to try to find out some reasons for people doing yoga, how many people there are practicing some sort of yoga, how often it is done, and how many new individuals there are nowadays. Below are a few of the major reasons that were listed as the reason for taking up the practice of yoga.

- 78.3% do it for flexibility.
- 62.2% do it for stress relief.
- 59.6% do it to improve overall health.

There are over 6,000 yoga studios in the US alone, and now there are even many schools that are teaching children between the ages of 4–17 the practice of mindfulness and yoga.

The average age seems to be around 18–44, approximately 82.2% are women, 17.8% are men, and about 8% are children. It was stated by 40% of people who are over 50 years of age that they now eat healthily and exercise more because of the awareness of their bodies that yoga has brought to them.

According to the International Yoga Federation, there are currently over 300 million people all over the world who practice yoga.

- 44.8% beginners.
- 39.6% intermediate.
- 21.9% came back after taking a break.
- 15.6% expert/advanced.

## Day 6: Come to Your Senses

Many times, in life, we momentarily lose our minds. We cannot see anything, we cannot hear anything except for those negative things that we have already convinced ourselves of.

You must now try to get yourself to wake up from that dream of negative stories that distance you from what happened in the moments that you experienced. Wake up and smell that freshly brewed coffee!!

Most people do not come to their senses on their own, they usually do not wake up overnight, and all of a sudden, think rightly. Usually, something drastic has to happen for us to wake up and see things for what they are, or make the changes that we need to make.

We have all said or heard someone else say that he has truly lost his mind! And in many cases, we now know that it is true. A lot of us temporarily lose our minds, and sometimes it is not that easy to get back in touch with yourself or your mind.

What if the whole world lost its mind all at once, where would we be? That is a scary thought. Even though some people believe that is exactly where we are right now because it looks like everyone has lost their mind, and they are not even trying to get it back.

The bottom line is that it is not easy to come to your senses without practice and continual practice because we're definitely out of shape and terms of that type of mental exercise and recognizing our relationship with those aspects of body and mind that work together

We are also out of shape and terms of perception and awareness, not physically. We get back in shape by going to a gym or another type of facility to physical exercise.

But we are aware of seeing the relationship between our conscious and what is available to be seen. We normally believe, and we think what is usually right in front of us, but even that is filtered through various unconscious thoughts.

We can see something but at the same time, not see what's important or relevant directly concerning our life and our well-being. Many times, we do not see things that we should see at all. Most of the time, it will be right under our nose or directly in front of our eyes.

We are running around operating on automatic pilots and do not take the time to see things for what they are, even when they are so close that they could slap us in the face.

You can be in a relationship for a year without really seeing the person for who they are because your thoughts about them have been dominated by your experience or by your fears. So, you never really see them for who they are. You see them for whom you need them to be, who you are comfortable with them being, or who you think they are.

A perfect example is how we live directly in nature, and we barely see that for what it is. We live in this beautiful natural world, but most of the time we don't notice it. We miss out on the sunlight, the stars, the birds, the trees, and everything else beautiful that we are surrounded by. But we are too caught up in what we call living life.

We can be easily programmed to see things in certain ways, and therefore we will never see things in other ways simply because of that direct programming.

## Day 7: Activate Your Senses

Aromas are a great way to relieve stress because it immediately activates your sense of smell, and that will do something positive to your spirit. Listen to your favorite song, especially if it is peaceful and inspiring; it will positively activate that sense of sound.

How about the smell of your favorite food from when you were a child, like the aroma of your grandmothers' apple pie or a freshly baked chocolate cake. That will automatically make you feel good because it is going to activate a positive memory from your childhood.

## Day 8: Have More Confidence

On your 8th day of meditation, you should start to feel more confident and more comfortable in your routine. We are going to take it one step further and you are going to try to incorporate Mindful Observation into your day.

Before you begin the practice of your meditation of choice, we are going to try a mindful observation exercise. Select an object in your immediate area, ideally something organic like a plant, insect, or fruit. Begin to watch the object as if you were looking at it for the first time. Don't do anything else except notice the object you are watching.

Explore the object visually by focusing on its shape and formation. Allow yourself to be consumed by its presence. Try to connect with its energy and its natural purpose in the world.

Once you have completed that exercise, it is time to practice your meditation of choice.

Try to practice mindful observation throughout your day after this meditation session. Make note of details in things around you that you've never noticed before.

At the end of day 8, document if you feel differently. Do you find meditation getting easier or harder? Is your current routine working for you? Do you feel like you have developed good meditation habits?

## Day 9: Meditation Routine

Begin your day with your meditation routine. We are going to take meditation even further by extending it to other areas of your life. It is important in your meditation journey to accomplish activities like mindful observation, eating, commuting, and working.

Begin your meditation as you usually would. Make sure you are still maintaining good posture, habits, and technique. Incorporate a mindful observation exercise at the beginning or end of your meditation. Choose a different object this time.

When you've finished your meditation, keep in mind that throughout the day you will be practicing mindful eating, commuting, and working.

To practice mindful eating, isolate a 15-minute block for one meal of your day to sit down by yourself to eat. Avoid any distractions that could arise like; other people, televisions, computers, and moving around. Plan to serve your meal on a plate or bowl. If you know you will be purchasing takeout, bring a plate or bowl with you. Make a conscious effort to chew your food properly. Stop eating when you feel about 80% full. If you are feeling stuffed during your meal, you have overeaten.

Next, we will practice mindful commuting. Pick a place that you will need to go to that day. This could be to work, to the grocery store, or the gym. If you are driving, make sure there are minimal distractions. Turn off any music or radio and begin to focus on the act of driving itself. If you are using public transit, avoid listening to music or scrolling on your phone. Pay attention to your environment. Observe the people around you and listen to the noises in your surroundings. You should immediately start to feel differently in this commute.

Lastly, we will extend your mindfulness to working as well. Pay attention to the work you are doing and try to think outside the box. Instead of rushing through things, try to think about them more deeply. Try to notice if this is helping with any stress or anxiety that you normally feel while working.

At the end of the ninth day of meditation, remember to document your findings. What was it like to practice mindfulness throughout the day? How did it feel to eat mindfully? What things did you notice during your commute when you were being mindful? Do you feel more at peace with yourself? Are you enjoying meditation?

## Day 10: Try Other Trying Mindfulness Exercises

On our last day of meditation, I want us to focus on another day of practicing mindfulness exercises. You have now accomplished a week of having continuous sessions of meditation, trying mindfulness exercises, and documenting your findings. The goal of this day is to incorporate these exercises into your everyday life.

As usual, begin your day with your regular meditation session. If you have the time, you may add a whole other session just to the mindful observation practice. You may multitask your mindful observation exercise with your mindful commuting exercise if you are tight on time.

Next, block off another 15 minutes in your day for mindful eating. If possible, challenge yourself to do this at every meal. If you are eating a meal with another person, invite them to try mindful eating with you. This can lead to a good discussion of the food and how it tastes or feels.

Practice mindful commuting whenever you have to go somewhere. Try to get used to doing this whenever you are driving, walking, or using public transit. If you are walking you can also practice mindful observation of the surrounding nature.

When you are working, try to be mindful of the entirety of it. This has been proven by multiple studies to reduce stress. Since most people are working for atlas eight hours of the day, being mindful during all that time can help to achieve inner peace and better mental wellbeing.

At the end of day ten, do some self-reflection. Think back to the beginning of your meditation journey. What changes do you feel? Do you feel a decreased level of stress, anxiety, and depression? Are you able to practice self-love more easily? Have you begun to notice the beauty of the world around you? Do you feel more at peace with yourself? If you answer yes to atlas one of those questions, it means meditation is already beginning to help you. Grasp onto that success as a milestone and don't give up.

# Chapter 7: Meditation for Anxiety

Meditating means becoming, evolving, transforming, and avoiding the emotional stagnation and stagnation of our thoughts. And to do this, we need to focus all our attention on the present moment, without distractions.

Meditation is just that: concentrating on the here and now, without anxieties, worries, and unnecessary thoughts. Meditating means enjoying the present moment and disciplining the mind to detach itself from its "autopilot" to contemplate what surrounds us and feel all the sensations that run through our body in the present.

Many have a distorted idea of meditation, and for this reason, I want to clarify what meditation is not before starting, to debunk the most common myths and wrong expectations:

## Meditation Is Not a Religious Practice

Although it has been used for thousands of years in various religious rituals and is akin to prayer in many respects, meditation is born much earlier than religions, and meditation practice itself is in no way connected to sacred rituals. The only point in common is the rediscovery of one's spirituality, even if divorced from the religious aspect.

Meditation is not a method to induce mystical visions or give us superpowers: no matter how fascinating the stories of the masters who managed to reach enlightenment effects that can only be reached after a lot of practice and in any case not guaranteed.

Meditation should not be addressed at all by expecting to be hypnotized or to be able to levitate in the air, because this would do nothing but get upset and deviate from the true purpose, rendering our attempts to meditate vainly.

## Meditation Is Not an Occasional Practice

To be able to see the first results, it is very important to be consistent and meditate every day even for just a few minutes, without ever skipping the daily meditation. Patience and perseverance will always have to accompany you, and I guarantee you that the results will come by rewarding your waiting.

Starting from these assumptions, below, I will list the precious techniques that I learned about meditating, easily applicable even by those who have never tried to immerse themselves in meditation before now.

# How to Meditate: Simple Techniques to Start Meditation

### Stop It All

Stopping is a term that reconciles little or nothing at all with the newspaper, as it demands that our world of "action at all costs" be silenced. To meditate, one must stop.

Search your daily life for the best moments to stop the inputs coming from everywhere to your brain.

Do you walk to work doing the usual route? Turn off the phone and walk without thinking about anything in particular, automatically take the daily roads and you will see that after a few days' things come to mind that have nothing to do with what you have to do these are also the cardinal principles of walking meditation. This process can be applied to any routine activity you do, including housework.

It often happens that during active work, concentration is lost and it is very difficult to re-start the plan. In this case, we advise you to try the so-called "stop-meditation." Whatever you do and whatever you do, stop for ten seconds and try not to think absolutely about anything (or concentrate on some subject).

A few moments of inner silence will lead you to greater clarity and help you tune in to work. Try it now! Reading this text—stop, look out the window, breathe calmly, follow your feelings, behold!

These exercises are a very effective way to deal with stress. This system of exercises is aimed at the interaction of the mind and body.

### Focus on Your Spirituality

We all have a spirit but is often suffocated by all the daily atrocities that engulf us and oppress us. Learn to give importance to words. When you hear, pronounce, read or think of a word, analyze it, discover its true meaning, check if it is used in the right way, learn to give it its real value.

Here, for example, the term value that I have just used can be a good example: what is the value? What do we value? Screen a day on a word of your usual language, a spiritual analysis of that term, and you will see how many things will appear different to you.

### Stop the Mind on an Object

We have so many things, we would like many more, but do we ever stop to look at what we have? Or just because they are our property, do they lie in a corner waiting to be dusted or recovered from the bottom of a drawer?

When you come home, take a moment and let your mind wander while you caress that object.

### Consider the Essence of Things

Do you remember that object you have been observing and touching for a few days? Now try to imagine its origins, how it is made, the materials used, who can have worked it and handled it.

As I write this chapter, I turned my gaze to a small jar, the transparent ones you buy when you travel. Inside, someone, with various layers of sand, has created a really beautiful landscape to look at, but I think of that sand collected on a beach overseas, to that person who touched it, sieved it, colored it. With technique and infinite patience, he created the sensation of waves, sails, seagulls, sun, sea.

I am in touch with his time, with his places, and this object transports my mind to other civilizations, through space and time. If you succeed and draw all this from an object, imagine when you will arrive at the essence of people!

## Investigate the Nature of Things

We learned a lot about food. We know how to read labels, origins, calories, we know that it is fundamental for our health, for our life, but do we know how to savor it? Do we understand its origins beyond the label?

Take a fruit, hold it in your hands and take the reverse path, think of the tree, the earth, the sun that has matured it, the care that was needed in the previous months to complete the cycle. Now eat it, savor it slowly, think that this taste will turn into energy, and you will be able to appreciate and enjoy what was trivial until yesterday.

What we've done so far is very little if you think about it. It didn't take your time; it didn't scratch your habits that much. Nobody noticed anything, while day after day through these constant exercises, you learned how to meditate and became aware of awareness.

## Think of the Consequences

Once awareness is reached, it is natural to think about the consequences. Every action, every word, every gesture, every single choice or of a society inevitably leads to consequences. Consequences that can be positive or negative and that in turn will trigger increasingly complex mechanisms.

It is not easy to understand this advice, above all, it is not easy to follow it, but those who want to approach meditation to know that it is a long and painstaking job to investigate within ourselves.

Think of the consequences that may derive from your response, from a stance, from your gesture.

I'm not suggesting you not do it, just think of the consequences first. Sometimes it can help you empathize, put yourself in the shoes of those who are receiving your answer or your gesture and think about how you would feel if you were in his place.

### Look for Harmony

We all have in mind the tremendous discomfort of the chalk that screeches on the blackboard or those deafening whistles that come out of the speakers while setting up an audio system. They are disharmonious sounds, the traffic noise is disharmonious, the screaming people are disharmonious, and I could go on forever.

We need harmony, and we need it as medicine. So we have to learn to create it.

Search for your place where you feel good. Create it at home, in your corner, or if you love walking, choose a forest, a river, in short, a place where you can take off all the superstructures and spend some time in peace and harmony. Make tea, surround yourself with elements that can create well-being, and try to spend at least 10 minutes a day, clearing your mind of everything that has happened to you. Just do it for yourself; it's a mandatory cure. Because to be able to give you must first find out what you have.

### Breathing "One-Four-Two"

Everyone knows that slow, deep breathing helps to relax and calm. Find a quiet secluded place where you can stay for 5–10 minutes, sit in a comfortable position, close your eyes, and put your hands on your knees. Watch your breath. Breathe measured and easily, letting go of all your thoughts.

Inhale into the count of 1, then hold your breath for 4 seconds, and exhale slowly into the count of 2. Continue to breathe in this way for 10 minutes, and your body and mind will come to a peaceful state. If there is such an opportunity, turn on meditative music, this will help to relax and concentrate faster.

It is important to note that to stay calm all the time, it is necessary to practice relaxation techniques regularly. Yoga classes can help.

### Body Recognition Meditation

Inside each person lives a whole cosmos that is constantly evolving and improving. At this very second, all sorts of chemical and biological processes take place in us, following which would be very interesting and informative. To quickly relax, find a secluded place, sit down, or reclining (just not too comfortable not to fall asleep) and begin to be aware of your body from the top of your head to your fingertips. Try to feel each cell, each hair.

Feel the warmth, relaxation, and tranquility that completely envelops your body. This relaxation technique promotes a surge of strength and energy. By the way, if you want to relax as quickly as possible, go for a massage.

### "I Am the Building From Which People Exit"

Sometimes, too much energy of all kinds accumulates in us, which can have a very negative effect on health if it is not released on time. To do this, imagine: you are a building at the end of the working day, and people leave you (people are a metaphor for feelings, emotions, stress, fears). They come out from everywhere, from all the "cabinets of you," from all the "windows of you."

They come out, and you remain empty. And you are cool, pleasant, comfortable. You are calm. This interesting technique can be used not only at home in a cozy atmosphere but also at work, giving yourself a 10-minute break and closing your eyes. Regular practice of this technique will help you to be balanced and not experience serious stress at work.

Do you know about the existence of a complex of therapeutic respiratory and physical exercises? After these, you will be able to feel better, both in body and soul.

### Conscious Location in Here and Now

All spiritual practices aimed at relaxation, emphasize the need to always stay in the present moment "here and now." Try using this technique to relax. To do this, you need to sit on the floor or in a chair. Paying rapt attention to the drive of your breath.

When you inhale, know that you are inhaling, and watch your sensations. Do this throughout your practice, constantly focusing on your breath. Or you can focus on the thoughts and feelings that arise in your body.

Interesting: to stay in the present, you can also help Thai massage with yoga elements, including deep muscle stretching and activation of the joints.

### Domestic Smile

All types of meditation have a positive effect not only on the person who practices this but also on his surroundings. People feel positive emotions, love, kindness, and are automatically drawn to all these wonderful sensations. So, the "Inner Smile" technique contributes to the greatest degree to the appearance of joy inside a person and has a beneficial effect on the world around him.

To do this meditation, you do not need much time, and it is enough to retire for 10–15 minutes, it is convenient to sit and close your eyes. Being in the most comfortable position, imagine that a bright, sunny light is spreading inside you, filling every organ, every vessel, every capillary of your body with the energy of love, a smile, and happiness. When you regularly repeat this practice, this energy will flow through you,

Surprisingly, creativity also helps to relax and gain inner balance. Go to a master class on a drawing in the sand and see for yourself.

# The Benefits of Meditation

Meditation is a psychic phenomenon that, using various techniques, is usually used to obtain states of relaxation in the processes of self-knowledge or the field of spirituality. It is based on careful consideration of something and is associated with concentration and deep thinking.

In the field of psychology, it is used, among other purposes, to analyze and generate cognitive changes and, if necessary, to relieve stress, anxiety, and other physical symptoms that allow you to achieve a certain state of psychophysical well-being through the control of thoughts and emotions.

### Introspective Meditation Therapy

The usefulness of this meditation therapy is the favor of introspection, understood as a mental process based on observation and analysis that a person makes from his thoughts and himself to find out his mental states, interpreting and qualifying his own cognitive and emotional processes, according to psychologist Philip Johnson-Laird (1988):

"Being able to be aware of ourselves is like becoming an observer of our actions, thoughts, and emotions, in such a way that we can change our way of acting, thoughts or controlling feelings."

Following the idea of the German psychologist Wilhelm Wundt that introspection is a reflexive means of self-knowledge to explain the etiology of current experience, it is a practice that can be applied to everyday life experiences that generate emotional disturbances and threaten our psychological well-being. It would be about observing ourselves as we live in an alarming situation.

## The Benefits of Meditation to the Mind

At some point in our everyday life, an event that changes our state of psychological well-being and becomes an anxious experience (personal conflict, accident, sentimental gap, etc.) may occur unexpectedly and unpredictably.

Knowing this experience, how we perceive it, and how to deal with it, is a fundamental step for the correct solution of this problem, because it is difficult to solve the problem if we do not know its basic elements. One of the benefits of introspective meditation is that it allows us to know the following elements to solve the problem:

- **What annoying bodily sensations I feel and make me feel bad?** We become aware that we are suffering from a psychological disorder when we notice certain bodily symptoms (the fact that our heart beats faster, our mind becomes numb and cloudy, our stomach contracts, etc.) as a result of the activation of physiological processes (thus reflecting the direct relationship body-mind).
- **What is the reason why I feel so?** Why does an external or internal stimulus (event, thought) become a source of anxiety and cause a series of unpleasant and irritating bodily symptoms?
- **What should I do to restore psychological stability?** It is about deciding how to deal with this, that is, choosing the right behavior in such a situation.

To find answers to these questions, meditation is based on 2 cognitive abilities: metacognition, defined by John Flavell as "knowing yourself regarding the cognitive processes and the products themselves or everything that is associated with them"; and meta-emotion.

## Psychological "I" in Meditation

Based on the psychobiological approach and taking into account that, through meditation, we take ourselves as subjects of analysis (in addition to the role of observer or researcher), the main problem is to determine the concept of "I" used here, without prejudice to the wide variety of concepts used in others areas:

"I am a psychological entity that changes in its state of equilibrium when it is affected by a stimulus that disturbs such a state."

It is easy to see that 3 factors interfere in a psychological disorder: body sensations are unpleasant, the emotional charge, and subjective knowledge of an alarming experience.

These factors are the result of 3 processes: physiological activation, unconscious mental processing, and conscious processing. Due to this difference, the psychological ego can unfold in 3 dimensions that perform different functions and can be attributed to 3 different psychological structures, each of which is guided by its mental program (in this sense, psychologist Victor Frankl and philosopher Max Scheler when they talk about a person and his genuine confrontation with suffering, they recognize the man as a 3D being in various modes of existence, such as biological, psychological and spiritual).

We can distinguish between:

- **Biological dimension:** associated with the physiology of the internal environment, the physiological self, this tells us that I feel what is happening inside our body, but does not develop value judgments.
- **Unconscious psychic dimension:** emotional self, which gives meaning and a general and quick assessment of what is perceived and reacts following it, activating the emotional system, which will contribute

to the appearance of irritating bodily symptoms.

- **Conscious mental dimension:** The self-conscious self, which evaluates broadly and concisely how I live in a situation and its consequences, and selects an appropriate answer. This is the dimension responsible for meditation, metacognition, and meta-emotion.

## Psychological Measurements

Following this approach, we will try to analyze the 3 dimensions mentioned:

### Physiological Measurement

It provides information on the physiological processes that occur in our body through the mechanism of interception that through the representation of the organs of our body unpleasant bodily symptoms are revealed: mental disorders, cardiac arrhythmias, nervous, sweating, stomach discomfort, etc. that occur from disorder.

The brain structure that is responsible for this function is located in the diencephalon (hypothalamus, pituitary gland, etc.). Interception is a neural system that promotes homeostasis, which performs the analysis of visceral information (digestive and genitourinary tracts, cardiovascular and respiratory systems), vascular pressure receptors, temperature and chemical solutions, and nociceptors located in deep tissues (muscles and joints) and surface (skin).

### Unconscious Mental Dimension

Our mind quickly, spontaneously, and unconsciously processes the perceived information about the situation, interpreting it and classifying it as unfavorable, offensive, harmful, unfair, aggressive, etc., and the result of which is the activation of emotional anxiety (prefrontal cortex and structures of the limbic system: tonsil, hippocampus, insulin, etc.) that cause the appearance of unpleasant bodily symptoms that interfere with this function.

The connection of perception with emotions is undeniable, as W. James (1884) has already pointed out: "A certain event produces emotions associated with physiological perception. In the absence of such a somatic perception, the main consequence will be the absence of any effective reaction."

### Conscious Mental Dimension

The self through meditation focuses on the experience of the moment. It processes information with accuracy and detail, paying attention to a greater number of factors. He uses reasoning (logical, heuristic, etc.) and functional or working memory to find out the circumstances associated with the event, its consequences, and future consequences, having as fundamental basis objectivity, that is, assuming that things are similar they are not so as we see them.

This will allow us to find out what the emotional signaling system has activated, why we "perceive" ourselves as sad, distressed, painful, embarrassed, shameful, melancholy, irritated, etc., and why, due to this emotional state, we decided on a specific answer to this situation (submission, revenge, forgetfulness). According to a neurologist, our emotions are the basis of our decisions, and this makes us a more desirable behavior than another.

The "I" preferably works through the prefrontal cortex, which is the only part of the brain in which information about the internal world of the body converges with information about the external world, creating a complex mechanism for representing our internal states.

# Chapter 8: Wading off Pain With Meditation

Relaxation, which may seem like a simple concept, can sometimes be hard to achieve, especially with individuals who suffer from chronic pain. Relaxation involves being able to take your mind off things such as the pain you are experiencing or the trigger causing anxious feelings and stress. Relaxing taking your mind off the pain can significantly reduce pain levels in the body and reap mental and physical benefits even when done for a few minutes. Relaxation can be anything from breathing exercises and meditation to painting or gardening. Whatever method you choose to employ in the attempt of relaxation should reduce stress by helping you ease built-up tensions in the body and reduce pain, thereby improving overall body wellbeing.

Lately, some pain relaxation techniques such as guided imagery, relaxation, breathing techniques, progressive muscle relaxation, music, massages, and stretches can help with labor pains by giving the brain a source of positive distraction. This, in turn, stimulates the release of endorphins in the body, rewiring your brain to think of the pains as productive, manageable, and positive.

Did you know that one breath could count as meditation? You probably didn't, but that's okay. I am here to explain what I mean by that in a simple manner. The way that you breathe has a bearing on how your body responds. If you panic, you may have noticed that your breathing becomes labored and you take in too much oxygen. The offshoot of this is that your pain levels get worse. The added oxygen in the bloodstream triggers that feeling of panic as your body tries to fight back thinking that you are in imminent danger. The air that you breathe goes down into your system and there is some truth in the fact that most people don't use the extent of their lungs during their breathing. We breathe in a shallow way and sometimes even find ourselves struggling for breath because we have forgotten to go through the motions. We are simply too busy with our lives to take much notice of that one thing that keeps us alive: the breath.

The exercises in this chapter help you to get back to basics because if you practice breathing every day in the manner suggested, you are helping your inner workings to do their jobs properly. Your sympathetic nervous system, for example, has multiple jobs to do within the body. If enough oxygen is not sent to the muscles in the body, we may find that we suffer from stiffness, which in itself causes pain. If you learn to breathe properly and feed the sympathetic nervous system with the right mixture of air at the right temperature, it can function in a better way and the air reaches all the parts of the body it was designed to reach. Over the centuries, mankind has changed many habits and the modern era hasn't helped much. We don't move enough. We are quite happy to allow our body to rest, but it's a good idea to get up and walk around because this also helps to distribute all the good things that your body needs.

I want you to breathe in deeply any way you feel and count in simple terms as you do so. I wouldn't mind betting that your inner breath counted up to something like 7 and you forgot to count your outgoing breath. You may even have breathed through your mouth. The reason that we have filters in the nostrils is so that the air that we breathe gets to the different body parts filtered of impurities and at the right temperature and that makes a difference to how your body responds. Many smokers, for example, have stopped breathing through the nostrils and now breathe through the mouth and that's a habit you may need to stem if you want to make the most of the meditation process.

## Exercise #1: The Body Scan

This is particularly useful if you suffer from chronic pain because you are already aware of your body and it will seem like second nature. The only thing that will be different is the way that you breathe and I am teaching you this first because this is the kind of breathing that you will do when you meditate.

Make sure that you wear something that isn't tight in any way. You need to feel totally comfortable, or as comfortable as you can be. Lie down on the bed and only use one pillow instead of the usual 2 because this opens up the airways and enables you to breathe better. Place one hand on the upper part of your abdomen because you will be able to observe what happens when you breathe correctly. The room should be fairly cool and have a good amount of air. Thus, if you are not accustomed to airing your bedroom, it's a good idea to start. The fresher the air, the more you get from the exercise. Close your eyes and start by breathing into the count of 7, out to the count of 9. Repeat this over and over again concentrating only on your breathing. As you do this, you will feel your hand rise and fall and this means that you are doing it right. If the movement of the upper abdomen tells you that you are breathing insufficiently and you should try to cause a pivoting motion when you inhale and exhale through the nostrils.

Now, think of your toes. Imagine that they are stressed and tense them and then relax them so that they are totally heavy and relaxed before moving on to the next part of your body, all the time breathing in the same rhythm as before. (7 in and 9 out). Now, move to your ankles and do the same. The idea is that you work through all the parts of your body, tensing that part that you are concentrating on and then relaxing it, so you work your way up to your legs to your waist, then up to your shoulders, and down to your hands, up to your arms, to your neck and then to the parts of your head.

During doing this, try not to think of anything else. Of course, you will, but don't beat yourself up if you find that thoughts creep in. Simply go back to your relaxation exercise and start again at the feet.

# Exercise #2 Alternate nostril breathing

For this exercise, sit in a hard chair, such as a dining chair, and place your feet flat on the floor. Your back should be straight. Breathe, in the same way as you did when you were lying down so that your upper abdomen moves with the movement of air through your body. This is a good exercise to do if you simply want to clear your mind of negative thoughts. When you are in a lot of pain, this type of breathing can help you to have something else to concentrate on until the panic passes. By breathing in this way, you are calming the inner you and that's important.

# Exercise #3 Self-Talk

This like transcendental meditation involves repeating a mantra, quote, or positive affirmation about oneself and the pain they are experiencing. For instance, instead of paying attention to the fact that one may not be able to finish their tasks in time due to some certain pain one can relax and remind themselves continuously that "no harm will come to anyone if I don't finish my task on time, but I can get a lot done by taking it slow."

# Exercise #4 *Vipassana* Meditation

Sit in a quiet place and observe your breathing while maintaining an equal state of mind (without trying to control it and just simply being aware). Whenever thoughts and pain arise, simply be aware of them and notice them without wishing for another experience or trying to push the experience away. Think of this experience as a passing cloud understanding that everything is impermanent. This technique is similar to mindfulness meditation, which uses just about the same instructions to relax and calm your mind causing pain and tension relief.

# Chapter 9: Getting Some Sleep

## Meditation to Overcome Insomnia

Whether you find it difficult to sleep at night as a result of stress, tiredness, work, or several other factors, or you find your sleep unsatisfactory, you might be suffering from insomnia. Insomnia is commonly called difficulty falling asleep, or staying awake, and there 2 types of insomnia.

Acute insomnia is mostly caused as a result of lifestyle, or circumstances. A security officer on night duty will find it difficult to fall asleep on duty, likewise, a first-time dad may find it difficult to fall asleep thinking of his precious wife in labor.

While chronic insomnia is a complicated type of insomnia. There is no known underlying cause, yet the individual finds it difficult to either fall asleep or sleep at night for long hours. Such a person may also experience disrupted sleep, more than 3 times a week.

Experiencing insomnia regularly causes mood disturbances, fatigue, stress, and difficulty concentrating. Although, insomnia can be caused by factors like anxiety, work-related stress, lifestyle, and sicknesses, the approach to overcome insomnia is not easy for some persons, yet there is one possible way to overcome not just insomnia but enjoy a long, satisfactory sleep for the rest of your life.

## How Does Meditation Cure Insomnia

Meditation is a relaxation technique worth trying, which can help improve your sleep, make you fall asleep easily, and also make your sleep satisfactory, such that you wake up feeling refreshed. Meditation harmonizes the mind and body and also influences the brain and the way it functions. The effect of meditation on your mind and body is that you become calm, and relaxed afterward.

## Effect of Meditation on Insomnia

During meditation, the mind is focused on one thing, which prevents the mind from wandering. Your mind and thoughts are brought to the now moment during meditation. Hence, anxiety disappears and it becomes easier to fall asleep.

During the meditation, your mind and body are been connected, and they both become relaxed and calm, which helps you sleep as soon as you get in bed.

Furthermore, meditation helps boost the hormone called melatonin that regulates the sleep and wake cycle. Without stress, the melatonin level is usually at its peak at night to ensure you get a sound and restful sleep. However, in the presence of stress among other factors that causes insomnia, the melatonin level drastically reduces, thereby insomnia occurs. With meditation, the melatonin level increases because stress has been reduced, and the body is in a relaxed state.

## Meditation Techniques for Insomnia

If you want to experience an undisrupted sleep, intense meditation must be done frequently. There are different techniques of meditating for insomnia and understanding the process helps us to get started immediately.

### Cognitive Shuffling

Cognitive shuffling is a simple meditation technique that can be done alone. It is simply a do-it-yourself technique that shuffles your thoughts to sleep. Here is how cognitive shuffling works, when you lie on your bed, your mind is likely to be filled with different thoughts from your daily activities. You can be worried, and anxious about your bills, relationship, the next day's activities, such that you find it difficult to fall asleep. The effect of this shuffling on the brain is it tricks the mind to get into a dreaming state.

*Tips to Practice Cognitive Shuffling*

- Firstly, getting in bed is important
- Right there on your bed, avoid focusing your concerns. Let your deadline be, the bills, the complicated issue at work. Let it all be.
- Now that your mind is free from your fears and worries, create a new engagement like imagining objects, places, names, or movies to meditate on. You can imagine different things, like a teddy bear, a fish, a dog, the sky, the rainbow, or the ocean. Note that, the items you are imagining should not be threatening or scary. For instance, instead of imagining an ocean because you have the fear of water, you can imagine the rainbow or the sky with beautiful stars.
- Ensure your eyes are closed before you begin the cognitive shuffling

process.

- The process should be repeated if you are still awake until you run out of words.

**Sa Ta Na Ma (Mantra)**

Sa Ta Na Ma is a powerful meditation technique that works on the brain and its functions to reduce the risk of depression and other mental illnesses. It is a mantra that is usually recited in 3 voices; the singing voice which stands for the active voice.

The whispered voice stands for your inner voice, and the silent voice is known as your spirit's voice.

SA TA NA MA chant describes the evolutionary aspect of the universe. Each word in the chant has a meaning.

- SA means the beginning.
- TA means existence and creativeness.
- NA means death or the end of life.
- MA means rebirth.

The effect of this mantra is displayed by a balance in emotions, and a settled mind.

*Practical Steps to SA TA NA MA*

- Find a comfortable position. You can sit down or lie down.
- Decide on how many minutes you want to recite the mantra.
- Breathe in and out through your nose and mouth and ensure you sigh after this breathing exercise is heard.
- Close your eyes properly, and place your hands either on your lap, or knee. Make sure your palm is facing up.

- Begin chanting slowly, and press the thumb of your hands, with your four fingers. Count your fingers each starting from the thumb to recite the mantra.
- Keep reciting the chant at a calm and slow pace During recitation, you have to follow the principles of the mantra.
  - When you mention SA, you count from your index to your thumb
  - You count from your middle finger to your thumb when you sing TA
  - You count from your ring finder to thumb when you recite NA
  - And finally, you should count from your pinky finger to the thumb when you mention MA.
- Still in that position, sing SA TA NA MA in a loud voice, your voice should be audible and ensure you move each of your fingers with each sound. The more you sing, the more you feel relaxed and energetic. However, your soul and spirit should feel relaxed and enjoy the sensation which is moving through your body and mind.
- When you feel relaxed, shift your focus and start singing in a whisper voice. At this point, energy is flowing through the body, waist, and knee.
- Next, be focused on silence. Continue counting your fingers and silently repeat the mantra to yourself.
- After singing the mantra completely, breathe in and breathe out with your arms wide open, and lift the hand above your head. Release your hands down, and exhale again. Repeat the process until you feel refreshed or drowsy.

# What to Expect When Meditating to Fall Asleep

Your expectations when meditating to fall asleep are most likely to have a sound and deep sleep at night, except you are uncertain about the benefits of meditation. Meditation for sleep is similar to another kind of meditation; however, the approach to each of these meditations is what matters.

When meditating, your meditation technique determines what you will have to do. Albeit, you can start preparing for your meditation exercise, by breathing in and out, lying flat on your back. If you are having a guided meditation, all you need to do is follow the instructions instead of been worried about what to do and what not to do.

Furthermore, all you should when meditating to fall asleep is sleep, but try to avoid any form of distractions.

## How to Meditate Before Sleep

There are 2 ways you can meditate before going to bed, one can be the practice of mindful meditation where you pay more attention to your body and mind, and also having a guided meditation where someone leads you through the process of meditation.

Mindfulness meditation can be done alone, in your room house. While guided meditation is a very easy meditation, it is just for you to follow and listen to instructions from a guide.

## Guided Meditation Tips for Insomnia

Guided meditation is the form of meditation you engage in with the help of a tutor or instructor. Ensure that you will not be disturbed, during this meditation.

- Lay down on your back, preferably on your bed or mat. Make sure you are comfortable with whatever you are lying on.
- Close your eyes and prepare your mind for the meditation you are about to engage in.

- Breathe in and out, ensure that your breathing out is audible such that it looks like you breathing out heavily. Make your body feel the heaviness, after which your body will be relaxed.
- Pay more attention to your breathing, and you feel easy. A natural breathing process.
- At this point, you will feel your body is relaxed. Feel the way your breath travels through your lungs, and hold your breath. As this is happening, you will begin to feel the relaxation in your body.
- You can begin to breathe normally right now, and as you breathe you feel your muscles, joints, and back relaxed.
- Pay more attention to your stomach area right now, where your abdominal muscles are present. Tighten the muscles in your abdomen, and hold your breath for 10 seconds and release your muscles. During this release, feel the difference in the tightness of your abdominal muscle and the relaxation of these muscles.
- Repeat the above process 5 times.
- Breathe in and out, tighten your abdomen and release it to relaxation.

**Feet**

- Divert your attention to your feet, and make them relaxed. The relaxation should be from your toes to your ankles. Tighten your toes and feet, and feel them become heavy and relaxed.
- Focus on your nails, feel them relaxed and let go.
- Pay attention to your thigh area, and feel them relaxed.
- Again, focus on your waist, lower and upper back, joints and feel them relaxed. You will feel the feet heavy, and very relaxed

**Upper limbs**

- At this point, focus your attention on your arms. Feel them heavy and relaxed.

- Get a sense of how heavy your arm is, and feel the relaxation shift to your elbow, wrist, and fingers become very relaxed.

## Face, neck, and facial muscles

- Shift your focus to your facial muscles, neck, and face.
- Every muscle in your face, your cheeks, and chin becomes relaxed, and your entire body is now relaxed.

## A deeper meditation for the abdomen

- Locate your center, which is your abdominal region. Imagine there is a ball on your abdomen. Slowly see the ball rolling over your abdomen area, and it relaxes every muscle the ball rolls in contact with.
- The ball now moves slowly from your abdomen area to your right hip carefully and softly massaging the muscles of the hips it comes in contact with.
- Massaging back and forth all the muscles in your abdomen.
- The ball continues to roll over to your knee, and around your knee. You can feel the tension on your navel melting away. Roll the ball slowly to your toe, and over to your toes, from your small toes to the big toes.

Every part of your body this ball comes in contact with feel the part of your body relaxing.

- Now feel the ball begins to roll upwards away from your toes again massaging and reducing tension around your toes, knees, ankles, and rolls over to your center, your abdominal area.
- Again, this ball rolls to your left thigh, and your knee, massaging both the back and front of your knee.
- With your ball, you move this ball to wherever you choose, and how

long you want it to be.

- With this ball, massage your knee, and ankle, and toes. This ball touches every muscle in your toes, it gently massages them and at this point, you feel your muscle relax.
- Feel the ball roll back up your leg, knee, and thigh muscle and arriving back at your center.
- Shift the focus of the ball to the base of your spinal cord. Allow the ball to rest there for 5 seconds, and allow it to move up your spine, and near your heart. At this point, you can feel the ball massaging the internal organs in your body. The ball massages the heart, and you feel relaxed.
- The ball rolls to your throat area, and the back of your neck area. You feel your neck area relaxing after the ball massages it. You feel the tension-reducing around your neck area.
- The ball travels down your arm, and to your wrist. The ball gently massages your wrist and fingers.
- You feel the ball roll up your arm, to your shoulder and neck. It travels down to your elbow, forearm, and wrist and into the palm of your hands.
- Allow the ball to gently massage your palm and fingers. The ball moves up your arm, shoulder, and face and as it reaches up in your face, the ball splits into a hundred tiny balls. You feel them travel around your face, to your eyes, eyebrow, cheeks, chin, tongue, and teeth.
- You feel the ball massaging your face and every part of your face. At this point, you should enjoy this facial massage.
- I want you to imagine as you are lying down the ceiling of your house. Your eyes are still closed, so imagine the ceiling of your room opening itself up, and the roof also opens itself open.
- Still looking at this opening, you will see the beautiful white sky. The sky is clear, bright, and the moon is out and also full, filled with stars. This is a magical peaceful night. You are alone, safe in this beautiful

part of your house.

- Watch the twinkling and beautiful little stars, looking down on you and you are enjoying the peace of the night.
- You look at the stars again, the little ones that are thousands of miles away are not shining so beautiful like the big star closer to you, that is looking at you directly from the sky.
- You are looking deep into the galaxy, beyond time, you see a million other stars waiting for you and shining at you.
- Take a deep breath. Breathe in a rich air from the infinite and beautiful galaxy filled with stars.
- Feel been a part of these stars, there is no separation between you and them. Feel you are already a part of this wonderful galaxy.
- As you experience this, you become a shooting star, shining across the galaxy like others.
- Slowly you begin to fade into the sky, into the unending space and galaxy.
- You are living in the wonders of this space, where there is neither time, past, or future. You feel you are the stars, the moon, and you occupy the space between the planets.
- You are floating off slowly, as you travel across this universe; you feel your body wants to drift away. You feel peace, wholeness, and love.
- When you are ready and feel relaxed, you can let go of the galaxy. When you drift off, you will drift into a peaceful and wonderful sleep.

# Chapter 10: The Future of Meditation

With the aid of technology, people who were once in doubt about the meditation practice are getting into it through guided meditations and apps that simplify things. People can now know when they are doing it right.

The internet has transformed the practice since one does not need to go find a teacher to learn. Instead, they rely on guided tapes and videos to learn the art. In this chapter, a little light is shed on the reach of meditation and the technology present.

## The Spread and Reach of Meditation

The practice of meditation is believed to have been going on well before written history. Its roots can be traced back to organized religious frameworks and beliefs in the East. It began its spread to Western culture in the 1960s and since then research on meditation has experienced tremendous growth as interest toward Eastern beliefs and philosophies has also grown. Since then, the rapid spread and expansion of meditation have been influenced by scientists, clinicians, theorists, health practitioners, and nonprofessionals who understand the practical benefits of meditation, especially in contemporary culture. These individuals and other meditators advocate for making meditation legitimate as a universal and non-sectarian practice as it unfolds many benefits and positive outcomes for mind, body, and soul, allowing us to experience the essence and fullness of life.

Over the past few years, meditation has achieved widespread popularity as one of the pillars of wellbeing alongside a healthy diet and exercise. Some people have even predicted that meditation will be among the next big public health revolutions. The trend has begun with promising positive results, especially in our current digitally addicted, demanding, and stressful times. The "Mindful Revolution" has taken the media by storm by announcing is the new focus-restoring and anxiety-attacking secret for everyone from government representatives to Silicon Valley entrepreneurs. This heavy globalization has also confused the practice and concept. The mixing of different meditation techniques as well has highly influenced the devaluing of the technique and can, in turn, begin losing its initial spiritual meaning.

## Meditation and Technology

Even with the spread of meditation, some people still do not meditate either due to lack of knowledge or due to lack of time. This was an opportunity for technology to come to do what it does best and make it easier for us to practice and manage. It began with the introduction of audio and videotapes for meditation, which made it easier to meditate as one did not have to go in search of a meditation teacher. The rise of the internet also gave a jump-start to the widespread making meditation more accessible to people from all over the world. Apps like *Headspace*, *Buddhify*, and *Calm* have made meditation easily accessible by allowing users to experience mindfulness with the ease of simply downloading an app and getting started. Apps are also currently developing to wearable technology such as the *Moodmetric* smart ring, which works with a mobile phone app to keep track of your stress activity, stressors, triggers, and relaxers.

# Chapter 11: Techniques to Try Out

Starting a meditation practice couldn't be less difficult. In its most essential structure, all you need is an agreeable seat, a cognizant personality, and to be alive. Pursue these means and become more acquainted with yourself better.

Locate a decent spot in your home or condo, in a perfect world where there isn't a lot of messiness and you can locate some tranquility. Leave the lights on or sit in normal light. You can even sit outside if you like, yet pick a spot with little interruption.

At the start, it sets a measure of time that is no joke "practice" for. Else, you may fixate on choosing when to stop. In case you're just starting, you can pick a brief span, for example, 5 or 10 minutes. In the long run, you can develop twice as long, at that point, perhaps as 45 minutes or 60 minutes. Use a kitchen clock or the clock on your telephone.

Numerous individuals do a session toward the beginning of the day and at night, or either. If you have the feeling your life is extremely occupied and you have a brief period, showing improvement over doing none. At the point when you get a little existence, you can do more.

Take a great stance in a seat or on some sort of pad on the floor. It could be a cover and a pad, even though there are numerous great pads accessible that will last you a lifetime of training. You may sit in a seat with your feet on the floor, freely leg over leg, in lotus pose, bowing—all are fine. Simply ensure you are steady and upright. On the off chance that the requirements of your body keep you from sitting upright, discover a position you can remain in for some time.

At the point when your stance is set up, feel your breath or some state "pursue" it—as it goes out and as it goes in. (A few variants of the training put more accentuation on the out-breath, and for the in-breath, you essentially leave a delay.) Inevitably, your consideration will leave the breath and meander to different places. At the point when you get around to seeing this—in no time flat, a moment, 5 minutes—return your thoughtfulness regarding the breath. Try not to pass judgment on yourself or fixating on the substance of the musings. Return, you leave, you return. That is training. It's frequently been said that it's straightforward; however, it's not that simple. The work is to continue doing it naturally. The results will accumulate.

## Posture

Posture is the primary factor in meditation—regardless of whether we choose to meditate while strolling. The stance is regularly dismissed by apprentices and the individuals who meditate without an educator. A skilled contemplation instructor will never give the poor a chance to pose slides. Stance shields the body from encountering torment, from the ill-advised arrangement, notwithstanding setting up the body for a meditative state.

- Take your seat. Anything that you're perched on—a seat, a

contemplation pad, a recreation center seat—discover and detect that gives you a steady, strong seat; don't roost or wait.

- If on a pad on the floor, fold your legs easily before you. (If you as of now do some sort of situated yoga act, proceed.) If on a seat, it's great if the bottoms of your feet are contacting the floor.

- Straighten—don't harden—your upper body. The spine has a common shape. Give it a chance to be there. Your head and shoulders can serenely lay over your vertebrae.

- Place your upper arms parallel to your chest area. At that point, let your hands drop onto the highest points of your legs. With your upper arms at your sides, your hands will arrive in the correct spot. Excessively far forward will make you hunch. Too far back will make you firm. You're tuning the strings of your body—not very tight and not very free. What's more, it may not be as startling as you might suspect.

- Drop your jaw a little and let your gaze fall delicately descending. You may allow you to eyelids lower. If you feel the need, you may cut down them absolutely, yet it's not critical to close your eyes while ruminating. You can mostly let what appears before your eyes are there without focusing on it.

- Be there for a couple of seconds. Settle. Presently you can pursue the next breath that turns out. You've begun on the correct foot and hands and arms and everything else.

Customary meditation and yoga stances have been created more than a large number of years, to consolidate legitimate breathing with the perfect arrangement of the vitality ways, inside the body. Put resources into a decent sitting pad. If you're sitting erect and straight, it puts an overabundance strain on the tailbone. Indeed, even the strictest of reflection experts may experience many sitting pads through an incredible span.

# Patience

A significant advance toward appropriate reflection is to comprehend that contemplation requires persistence. It can take long stretches of committed everyday practice to arrive at the more profound degrees of awareness. A few people guarantee to have opened accessible routes to the more profound conditions of cognizance, yet these cases ought to be thought about while considering other factors.

Regardless of whether somebody built up an enchantment pill that could sling clients into the most profound thoughtful states, what great would it be? A significant portion of the reflective way is simply the adventure. Reflection requires some serious energy and practice. For specific individuals, it takes more time to clear the psyche than others. Much the same as Yoga don't compel it—simply make the most of your voyage.

# Breath

Breathing must be done appropriately, and a factor that disrupts everything for some people is a nasal blockage. The average individual can experience existence with their nasal sections swollen or blocked, and scarcely take note. In any case, a person who rehearses Yoga, or reflection, ought to be substantially more mindful of dissemination issues in their nasal locales. An extraordinary custom to perform, before contemplation, is nasal purifying. This should be possible, consistently, with a neti pot or sinus wash bottles, ensuring the nasal sections are clearly taken into account by breathing through the nose. It ought to be noticed that some nasal conditions may not clear up. In such a case, breathing through the mouth is the main choice, and there is no sense in agonizing over it.

# Atmosphere

Clearing up every single imaginable interruption, before ruminating, is another fundamental advance. Mood killer, the telephone, eat a little dinner in advance, so you are not only ruminating over being ravenous, and truly set the climate for the reflection session. On the off chance that you practice contemplation after Yoga asana practice, you may have an unfilled stomach, and your session may pursue an inflexible calendar. Never make progress toward flawlessness, since all flawlessness is, at last, a fantasy, yet do what you can to advance a thoughtful climate. Your reflection sessions will improve significantly if you let flawlessness go.

## Simple Meditation Techniques

Meditation is the act of utilizing reflection and breathing systems to incite smoothness and quietness. Individuals have polished meditation for many years, once in a while as a piece of strict articulation. Be that as it may, reflection isn't restricted to rigorous practice; indeed, a great many people use it just as an approach to adapt to pressure. Figuring out how to ruminate can improve your life and assist you with living every day without limit.

### Planning Space for Meditation

It doesn't make a difference where you reflect since you feel loose and quiet. A pleasant spot free of interruptions will enable you to focus. A few people accomplish this by darkening the lights, lighting candles, or consuming incense. Others favor a spot where they can feel the glow of the sun. There is no set-in-stone spot to reflect, similarly insofar as you're agreeable and ready to center.

Regular individuals reflect in an upright position, sitting with a straight back to encourage profound relaxing. This could mean sitting on the floor or in an agreeable seat. If you intend to sit on the floor, consider getting a yoga tangle for comfort. Oppose the compulsion to rests, particularly in case you're new to contemplation since you'll get drowsy and lazy.

## Breathing Techniques for Meditation

Breathing is key to meditation, so it's essential to see how to do it appropriately. To begin with, you ought to sit upstanding with your spine straight. Get settled, close your eyes, and take a full breath until your lungs feel full. You, as a person, need to withhold your very own breath for few seconds at that very point gradually breathe out. Ensure that you inhale through your nose and that you never secure your jaw as you relax.

At the point when you inhale, you should feel your stomach grow forward, and your ribs separate marginally. As you breathe out, attempt and spotlight on the sentiment of air leaving your body. A great many people discover this sensation unwinding, however, be careful with pressure on your shoulder and neck. From the start, it may be difficult to take as such, however, with training, it will turn out to be very agreeable.

## Quieting Your Mind for Meditation

Numerous individuals make some troublesome memories quieting down their psyche from the clamor of the day. Our lives are occupied to the point that the majority of us run throughout the day and breakdown into bed around evening time. For the day, we consider our work, companions, and family, physical checkups, school, and different commitments we may have. Releasing the entirety of what can be a major challenge.

One strategy you can use to quiet your brain is to just concentrate on the way toward relaxing. This system gives your mind something to focus on, which is more straightforward than attempting to consider nothing by any means. As you inhale, consider the entirety of the sensations you feel. If your mind begins to meander, recognize the idea and refocus on your relaxing.

# Instructions to Incorporate Meditation Into Your Martial Arts Training

Meditation has continuously assumed a significant job in combative techniques preparing. For the individuals who have never attempted to consolidate contemplation into their preparation, consider joining this antiquated system as you learn hand to hand fighting. Numerous experts of various styles propose a particular way to contemplate; however, you can utilize any strategy that you are alright with. Meditation, when used during preparing, is a perfect method to help achieve the engaged, quiet mental expression that is so critical to acing your battling aptitudes.

Meditation is regularly used even by individuals who don't rehearse hand-to-hand fighting as a method for adapting to the worries of their regular day-to-day existence. At the point when an individual practices meditation all the time, they find that their focus and attention to self as well as other people is extraordinarily improved. While the objective of contemplation is to loosen up the body and make a more advantageous body and soul, the training has numerous applications to the individuals who need to learn combative techniques. For a large number of years, professionals have utilized contemplation to help plan for the fight to come. Truth is told, by and large, the act of physical exercise is viewed as a type of contemplation in itself. Meditation is likewise viewed as a preparation that enables the brain to become as stable and snappy as the body.

Probably the best case of how meditation is utilized in combative techniques preparing is the investigation of *Tai Chi*, which consolidates mental fixation, centered breathing, and moderate body developments to improve wellbeing, diminish pressure, and make the body more grounded. Yoga is viewed as reflective military workmanship that is utilized to advance wellbeing, accommodate self-protection, and permit the individuals who learn hand to hand fighting to turn out to be all the more profoundly focused. This is one of the few styles that are intended to interface the body with the brain to improve center and coordination.

Similarly, as there are various hand-to-hand fighting styles, there is additionally an assortment of reflection procedures that can be utilized as you learn combative techniques. You might need to invest a little energy looking into the particular style you practice, and seeing whether there is a type of meditation that is regularly utilized close by it. If you are prepared to join reflection into your preparation, it is something that you can undoubtedly do at home. After you have invested energy preparing, move to a reflective stage.

Center your psyche, and go through 15 minutes rehearsing the individual moves or types of your order at a moderate pace, concentrating eagerly on the sentiment of your body and the elegance natural to the development. Slow your breathing, and let your mind center just around playing out every development flawlessly. While it might appear to be outlandish, acing these strategies at an extremely moderate pace will enable you to perform them faultlessly at max throttle when fundamental.

## How Aromatherapy Enhances Meditation and Yoga

Reflection and yoga are incredible assets to accomplishing entire body wellbeing. Yoga is an antiquated physical and mental practice.

Most yoga studios will finish up a class with *Shavasana. Shavasana* is the time you are urged to calm your psyche, interface with your body, and spotlight on reflection.

Joining the acts of yoga and meditation enables you to comprehensively better your psyche and body wellbeing. Meditation quiets the brain, alleviates tension, and is useful for heart wellbeing, insight, center, and memory. Yoga has more than 50 distinct advantages for physical, passionate, and emotional wellness.

The advantages of yoga and meditation are outstanding; to give some examples of significant favorable circumstances of yoga are: to incorporate lower circulatory strain, solid safe framework, enthusiastic steadiness, and honed concentration just to give some examples. Keep in mind the forces of meditation and yoga.

### Taking Your Practice to Another Level

To accomplish considerably more noteworthy outcomes from your training, you should take your yoga and meditation to another level. Including fragrant healing can help you in achieving a lot more elevated level of order, the more prominent your control, the better your outcomes.

### How Does Aromatherapy Work?

Fragrance-based treatment is the utilization of basic oils to advance a positive personality and body wellbeing. Fundamentals oils are gotten from different plants, blossoms, natural products, roots, stems, bark, and different botanicals.

These natural materials are significantly moved in fundamental oils, giving us a solid olfactory encounter. Oils animate the immensely significant feeling of smell and olfactory organs and afterward speak with the mind's recollections and feelings, or limbic system.

This sort of treatment is accepted to battle torment, sleep deprivation, melancholy, other states of mind, and that is just a peek of something larger. Essential oils have on a very basic level equivalent to purposes as yoga and meditation, so they look good as an extension to your preparation or training.

### Choosing Your Essential Oils

While choosing your essential oils, it is critical to think about your objectives in fragrance-based treatment. Various oils have different purposes, capacities, and impacts, and each is reasonable for its specific and explicit circumstance.

The treatment for one concern will change from that of another, similarly as an anti-infection would be utilized to treat a disease.

For example, an individual experiencing a sleeping disorder may utilize oils like lavender, vetiver, or chamomile, which are quieting and evoke the unwinding reaction in the body. Then again, a person who battles and fights with sluggishness would use oils like basil, eucalyptus, lemongrass, orange, or peppermint to incite imperativeness. By investigating essential oils and their points of interest, you can locate reasonable decisions for you.

### Strategies to Implement Aromatherapy

When you have investigated your basic oil choices and chose the correct oils for you, you are prepared for basic oil use and application. There are a couple of various ways you can include fragrance-based treatment into your everyday schedule. Here are some extraordinary choices so you can decide the best usage strategy in your customized practice.

- *Anointing:* Essential oils are profoundly kneaded onto the skin during extending or rest time; this can consider expanded perception and core interest. Never apply basic oil straightforwardly to the skin; it must be mixed with a bearer oil, like jojoba, canola, or olive oil.
- *Diffusing:* Using a fragrance-based treatment diffuser, essential oils are scattered all through the demeanor of your yoga space. This makes a specific mindset or environment for upgraded practice. Light lights are another way you can diffuse oils. They smell lovely, creating an alluring yoga and reflection space.
- *Purifying:* Essential oils are utilized as an astringent cleaning strategy. This freshens up and purifies the workspace. Add your oils to a splash bottle with water to start utilizing, splash to wash down, and refine your zones.

### Implementation

With the customary practice of meditation and yoga, you will just keep on advancing your physical and psychological well-being. Adding fragrance-based treatment to this standard will help you in surpassing your objectives.

Test the various techniques for actualizing fragrance-based treatment and investigate your basic oil choices. Test various items until you locate the correct recipe for your training. Regardless of whether you are a prepared yogi or a learner understudy, fragrance-based treatment will support the achievement and prizes of your control.

# Step by Step Instructions to "Yoga Meditate"

There is no uncertainty that yoga gives numerous medical advantages to its professionals, including a fortifying of the center muscles, expanded adaptability, and accomplishing better core interest. A significant piece of yoga that numerous novices don't exactly comprehend is the zone of yoga meditation. As your training develops you will find that there are multiple yoga meditation systems to ace. Yet, as an amateur, it is ideal to ace the nuts and bolts.

You may find that it is simpler to keep up a meditation state while focusing your eyes on a solitary article. Keep your eyes concentrated on that one article for the span of the reflection; this has a quieting impact on the brain. It is very difficult to remain loose and centered when you are glancing all around. Not exclusively will this assist you to get acclimated with the meditation; it will likewise improve your parity.

Breathing is fundamental to your yoga practice. Legitimate breathing will go far to helping you to expand your scope of movement, accomplish represents that you thought incomprehensible, and enable you to enter a more profound condition of meditation. Attempt to concentrate exclusively on your relaxation. On the "chance hit" that you discover your mind meandering, bring it back in and focus on taking in and out.

These 2 hints are progressively significant that you may understand. The foundation of any effective yoga practice and yoga reflection is proper breathing and looking after core interest. In the case that you go to an extremely live class, a teacher can work with you to advance these strategies. On the off chance that going to live preparing is beyond the realm of imagination, at that point, there are a lot of DVDs accessible.

In time you will find that yoga builds your quality and adaptability. It will likewise enable you to improve your quiet and allow you to manage unpleasant circumstances in a more loosened-up path than any other time in recent memory. You will find that circumstances that used to worry you or cause you tension to appear to be a lot prettier at this point! Yoga isn't the main thing that I see as unwinding. In all honesty, keeping a fish aquarium has to quiet and loosening up benefits too!

Thank you so much for reading my book.

I can't tell you how much it means to me that somebody chose to read something I created.

I hope you enjoyed it as much as I wanted to write it.

It takes much time, energy, and hard work to write the best possible result for your experience, which is why it would mean a LOT if you could take just two minutes from your day and leave a review on Amazon. It doesn't have to belong or be detailed – any comment will do.

Scan the QR Code and follow the simple instructions!

## CLICK HERE US REWS

## CLICK HERE UK REWS

If there's anything from the book you didn't understand or have any suggestions to improve the book, don't hesitate to contact me at the email address youbooks.editions@gmail.com and I will respond as soon as possible.

Many thanks for considering my request.

# Conclusion

Daily meditation practice can make you healthier, happier, and more successful than ever. Only a few minutes of meditation practice daily can help you lower stress, improve your mental and physical health, boost your focus and increase work productivity. If you heard about meditation but don't know how to begin—or you have practiced meditation in the past, but need help to get started again, this beginner's meditation guidebook is for you.

Whether this is your first experience with meditation practice, or you have practiced before, this book will transform your relationship with yourself and the world around you. This book opens the door to a life lived in the freedom of your innermost being. We hope that this book is going to help you to find the best method for mindfulness meditation, useful exercises, and practices, suggestions for relaxation, stress relief, and better sleep. We encourage you to try implementing meditation in your everyday life because we live in a stressful time and our mental and physical health could depend on it.

You may find benefit in learning to be a better-rounded individual with emotional intelligence, hoping to defeat your anxiety through learning social skills that can benefit you. You may find benefit in becoming more skilled at the techniques brought to your attention within this book. You may even prefer a book dedicated solely to cognitive behavioral therapy that can teach you the steps necessary to complete a cognitive restructuring in detail.

You deserve to live a life that is one you can enjoy, free from worrying about what your friends think of you. Through spending the time and effort necessary, you can achieve that life that, up until this point, may have seemed like an impossibility. It will not be easy, but it is possible for you. If you want it, all you have to do is reach for it and practice the steps provided within this book for you. With the effort necessary, you will begin to find relief from the symptoms, and if you do not, you are not out of options—a therapist or licensed medical professional can help you further. Just remember, there is always hope of getting out of this situation. All you have to do is ask for the help that is out there.

Edited in Europe, printed in the United States of America unless otherwise specified.

Guided Meditation for Beginners

Printed in Great Britain
by Amazon

11430729R00071